Campaigning in Zululand

Campaigning in Zululand

Experiences on Campaign during the
Zulu War of 1879 with the 94th (North
Worchestershire) Regiment

W.E Montague

LEONAUR

Campaigning in Zululand:Experiences on Campaign during the Zulu War of 1879 with the 94th (North Worchestershire) Regiment.

Published by Leonaur Ltd

Originally published under the title
Campaigning in South Africa

Material original to this edition and its origination in
this form copyright © 2006 Leonaur Ltd

ISBN (10 digit): 1-84677-101-3 (hardcover)
ISBN (13 digit): 978-1-84677-101-9 (hardcover)

ISBN (10 digit): 1-84677-092-0 (softcover)
ISBN (13 digit): 978-1-84677-092-0 (softcover)

http://www.leonaur.com

Publishers Notes

In the interests of authenticity, the spellings, grammar and place names used in this book have been retained from the original edition.

The opinions of the author represent a view of events in which he was a participant related from his own perspective; as such the text is relevant as an historical document.

The views expressed in this book are not necessarily those of the publisher.

Contents

Chapter One
Off to Fight the Zulus

The Zulu War came to us, as to many others, a sorrow and a surprise.

On the evening of the 11th February the papers had been full of accounts of the disaster of the 22d of the previous month at Isandlwana, and it was felt that England would make a great effort to retrieve that reverse; but that it should come home to us as individuals was not so clear.

Upon the morning which followed the receipt of the news, there was to be a "Brigade day," —the regiment was quartered at Aldershot,— and, after an early breakfast, I went up to barracks to take part in it. But instead of finding the companies standing on parade in readiness to be inspected, I found the men gathered in groups, not talking much,—just standing as if they had heard something, and expected shortly to hear more.

There were but a few minutes of suspense. On the orderly-room table lay the order for the regiment to be held in readiness "for immediate embarkation on service in South Africa." For the first time we were going to fight.

My wife met me in the entrance to our hut; it was unusual for me to return so early. Besides that, there must have been something in my face which had not been there before.

"We're ordered off to the Cape at once, Nelly!" I said. It was no time for begging one's words.

Nelly gave a slight shiver, and I saw her hand press on the handle of the half-open door she was holding, a trifle heavier than it had done before I spoke. That was only for a second,—little more. Then she gave a faint smile, and laid both hands on my shoulders, saying, as she kissed me, "I'm so glad, Ned, because I know that you are glad." And after that she burst out crying.

So the memorable news came to many houses on that

memorable day.

Then followed days of hurried preparation; journeys to town by the morning train, to return by the last one laden with parcels. White's shop in Aldershot became a fashionable resort: hardly was an afternoon passed without paying it a visit—something had been forgotten; and then you were sure to meet every one there.

The thing that impressed itself most upon my mind in those last days was the immense amount of lettering that was done in that shop. Every one going out ordered some dozen articles or more, and on each article had to be painted name, rank, and regiment of the owner. The painters sat in corners, opposite to piles of goods, working on endlessly, as it seemed. Buckets, pillows, canteens, valises, tubs, bags, caps, filters, tables, chairs, bedsteads,—all had to be lettered by those patient men. How they kept the things from getting thoroughly mixed was a puzzle.

Oscillating continually between the shop and barracks, always in a hurry, and laden with the smaller purchases, we, the lucky ones going out, were easily to be distinguished from the unlucky ones left behind, who walked slowly and carried no parcels. Poor fellows, how we pitied them!

The letter-rack in the ante-room could no longer hold our correspondence. When the rack was full, the circulars, books, letters, and other tradesmen's offers of assistance, overflowed on to the mantelpiece; that full, the writing-table was taken up; that covered, the floor received the rest. Chaos reigned supreme in the mess. Piles of letters addressed to officers who had long since left were heaped about. The newspapers lay anywhere, torn and mangled, —the mess sergeant was too busy to cut the leaves or sew them together. Parcels which had been opened, left their brown-paper wrappers in the corners. The fire was neglected, and often went out. In the midst of the confusion the mess property was sold by auction, and the rooms were infested by Jew purchasers anxious for their bargains. For the rest of our time we sat on three barrack-chairs, over a fire without a fender, in an empty hut, lighted at nights by a couple of candles.

Amongst other amusing incidents of the time was the arrival of three tailors, rivals, each anxious to supply us with uniform and helmets fitted for the climate of South Africa. They were small-sized men, unmistakably tailors, and when told to come in, did so with a timid air, as if expecting some rough practical joke from the officers who had need of them.

They halted inside the door, and drew up in a line. Then, as if by signal, each one unrolled his sample red coat, and held it up to view; flimsy, fluttering things, gaudy with gold lace, and about as unfit for campaigning as could be designed.

The things fluttered and glittered; above them peered the anxious faces of the three tailors; opposite were the officers looking rather bored. Eventually the boldest of the tailors spoke up, shaking his coat in our faces; and his effrontery gained him the day, and he received many orders.

On his delivering my own garments, I suggested, by way of a joke, that I supposed it would do if I paid him on my return.

"Why, sir, you see," was his reply, "when gentlemen are going out as you are, sir, it is always a case of ready money,"— a pleasant hint which reminds me of the view of Isandlwana taken by my bootmaker, a well-to-do gentleman in the West End, who shook his head over the news pathetically as he said, "Sad business, sir—very sad; nothing like it in England since I can remember. We lost three customers by it, sir!"

Another phase of the times was the arrival of men's fathers— or other near relatives—fine old fellows, with their eyes always following their sons' movements; trotting down into the town to bring back some small thing that might be useful; trying to chat unconcernedly with the rest as if they were down amongst us on a pleasure-trip, and as if the queer life they had suddenly tumbled into had been theirs during the last half-century. It was a hard time of discomfort for most of them, and the pangs of parting were rendered none the less bitter by the weary mockery of keeping up cheerful appearances when the hearts were full.

Meanwhile in the huts the men were being fitted with boots and clothes, accounts were feeing signed, sickly men picked out to remain behind, warnings given, threats or promises held out, anything to keep the men together under such exciting circumstances. Six hundred volunteers arrived,—men whose faces we had not seen before, and who had not seen each other's faces till they met on our parade-ground. A company, yesterday fifty strong, to-day expanded itself into over a hundred, and you walked down a double rank of strange faces peering curiously at you, and wondering what sort of a "cove" you were likely to prove by your looks. Added to all, it was bitterly cold weather—snow one day, and slush the next—thoroghly inclement, cheerless, and miserable. Then our boxes had to be returned to store, or packed for travelling, and we slept in the blankets meant for future use in Zululand.

There were farewell dinners to be eaten at neighbouring messes, speeches made and returned, when the champagne made hosts and guests equally feel heroes, followed by headaches and more packing in the morning.

On one of these last days the Duke of Cambridge came down from London to inspect the regiments for Africa. From an early hour the camp was alive with vehicles hired by parties of tourists and sight-seers. The sides of the parade-ground were lined with patient groups of that class of nondescripts who never fail to attend when anything is going on. They appear to belong to no particular set — mere idlers, with more time on their hands than they know how to get rid of, A tall, young-looking man, with curly hair, and a big coat profusely trimmed with Astrakhan wool, gained an entry into our desolate ante-room, introducing himself as the representative of the 'Daily Telegraph,' sent down specially to report on the day's doings. This was our first acquaintance with the ubiquitous "correspondent."

On parade we turned out in our white helmets, which gave the men a smart appearance, but looked sadly wintry against the leafless trees and snow-heaps. One desolate sub-lieutenant, destined to be left behind, wandered round the flanks of the companies, wearing one of the usual black-felt helmets, and looking as disconsolate as the Peri at the gate of Paradise. Mingled with sight-seers were piteous groups of ladies, intently watching our movements, and appearing to derive what little consolation was possible from the companionship of one another. Wives, mothers, and sisters gathered in quiet groups, taking a sad interest in those very dear to them, soon to be separated and lost to sight. After the "march past" the Duke took the officers on one side, and delivered a short speech, interrupted by an obtrusive "correspondent," who, note-book in hand, edged in behind us, only to be ignominiously turned away. The Duke looked older and more bent; his well-known face is puffier than of old, and the purple and red are creeping over it with unmistakable strides. He rode the handsome old roan charger which has been his favourite for years, and spoke earnestly and kindly, as is his wont.

"A little steadiness wanting, gentlemen; the 'march past' not all that can be desired: steadiness and drill are what are required. You have a regiment of young soldiers who have much to go through, and it is by steadiness and drill that you will do all you should. That it will be done so, I have no doubt; that every officer and man will do his duty when the time comes, is only what, as English soldiers, you will do, as others have done before you." To all of which we said a silent "Amen" and then the kind-hearted old soldier rode away, and we were dismissed.

My own hut looked empty and dismal enough without Nelly and the children. An officer and his wife had been to look at it, and the time of my departure was evidently a matter of deep interest to them. In the little dining-room—so small that Patrick, our soldier-servant, standing in the doorway, could hand the dishes pretty well all round the table—was my camp-bed, a portmanteau, the company's defaulters-book, and a pile of opened letters—some bills, others parting words from friends. Patrick, on his knees at the fireplace, was vainly trying to blow some life into the fire. Outside, the snow was falling and the dead leaves driving. The little gate we had put up to keep a neighbour's fowls out of the garden hung on one hinge. The gravel-walk was littered with straw from the packages, now carted away. Opposite, the regimental "wash-house" was closed, and the clothes-lines, till yesterday never empty, were gone with the soldiers' wives sent home; rather a mockery on

11

the word for those whose homes were broken up—the husband to fight in Zululand, the wife to find a scanty welcome with parents or sisters more pinched than herself.

Such was the outlook on our last day at Aldershot. On the morning of the next, late in February, we stood on parade for the last time, while the General of our Brigade addressed to us a few words of God-speed. The snow lay thick on the ground, and the men beat a dismal tattoo with their feet as the words came across the ranks:—

"Let every bullet find its billet in a Zulu's breast. You are leaving your sweethearts behind you, men: let each man's rifle be henceforth his sweetheart; let him cherish it as he would the girl he has left behind him." The sentiment called forth a good cheer. Then the band struck up, and we marched off to the station.

The sight-seers, were gone; but here and there stood those quiet groups of ladies, two or three together, tearless and brave, though their hearts were breaking. And as the "line" passed them, now and then a handkerchief would be waved, or a hurried embrace snatched as a last goodbye.

At the barracks the men turned out with three hearty cheers; an ovation continued throughout the town, making me feel that, for my own part, I would suffer a great deal rather than not deserve the confidence which so many of our countrymen showed in us.

Just when the cheering was at its height, and the "line" was surrounded by throngs of people crowding round to shake hands for the last time with their friends in the ranks, a small shop-boy struggled up to me, presenting a bill for one-and-eightpence, which he demanded of me to pay on the spot. Never was a case of disillusion more plainly illustrated—never did a more complete awaking from a dream take place. A moment before, my heart was beating high with heroism, longing for some forlorn-hope or desperate service with which to prove my devotion to my country; now, my only feeling was one of disgust, and a longing to kick the wretch trundling along by my side with his horrible "little bill."

12

Never was greater enthusiasm shown than on the occasion of the reinforcements starting for Natal. At Southampton the two trains conveying the regiment passed slowly through long line's of people, all shouting and cheering, the women waving handkerchiefs, and urging us on to go out and avenge our fallen soldiers. The dockyard was crammed; even the vessels lying alongside the *China*, on which we were to embark, were filled with spectators. Windows of the warehouses commanding a view of the ship were occupied by parties of ladies, while the gates leading to the landing-place were besieged by anxious crowds, all begging for admittance. So the afternoon wore away: the men were stowed below like so many sardines in a box; the officers snatched a minute now and again to consume bottles of champagne with their friends in the saloon; the old Duke paid us a flying visit, and at last we cast off from the quay, and steamed slowly past the dockhead. The crowds, there as elsewhere unmindful of the bitter wind, cheered and waved their handkerchiefs, while the band on board played "*Auld lang syne*" and "*The girl I left behind me*," till the men could blow no longer. Then more leave-taking as the steam-tender alongside blew her whistle; a rush to the gangway; and a few minutes after the order, "Full speed ahead," England was once more a thing of the past.

Chapter Two
At Sea

The *China*, like the *Russia*, is one of the Cunard Line, and proved an excellent and comfortable vessel, though now considered behind the age, and only runs across the Atlantic during the summer when an extra steamer is required. Everything about her denoted strength and safety. Her plates were a third thicker than those used in the construction of ordinary iron ships, while fittings and appointments were solid and old-fashioned. Anything required for the ship's fitting is supplied to the order of the chief officer, the Company considering that if a man is fitted for so responsible a post he is the best judge of the ship's requirements. Another excellent rule forbids the ship's officers to mix with the passengers. On a "Cunarder" there is. none of that lounging about in fancy costume by the side of the young ladies which is so conspicuous amongst the officers of many ocean lines. The captain alone dines in the saloon, taking it in turns to preside at the upper and lower tables, thus avoiding jealousies. The watch on deck is kept constantly at work night and day: thus there is none of that hauling men out of holes and corners on dark nights when a sudden call for them arises. This excellent rule had its disadvantages, as the silent hours of the night were continually disturbed by holy-stoning decks, or tramping after some rope, the hauling of which could well have been left till morning.

The table, supplied, from the ice-house throughout the entire passage, furnished a superabundance of solid food. No French cookery or "kickshaws" are allowed on so conservative a line goose, ducks, pork, colossal joints, huge hams, and thick rich soups appeared as regularly as dinner came round, filled in with smaller dishes in which the same meats, cut up and disguised with sauces, did duty as entrees. With these were a sprinkling of American dishes, with names strange to English ears. At lunch the invariable dish was stewed prunes, boasted by the Company to have been supplied at that meal without a day's interruption since its formation.

On the cabin-table lay an album, magnificently got up in crimson cloth and gilt edges, Containing the history of the Line—photographs of the steamers, plans of the cabins, rules and regulations, charts of the routes taken, and a series of amusing papers by popular well-known authors, describing their experiences on tours to America and other places to which they had journeyed by the assistance of the Company. These papers were not unlike the advertisements which appear in local papers from the "gentleman's tailor" or the "practical hatter," as the descriptions of scenery or travel invariably led up to the final "puff," cunningly hidden as the reader read it through, unwitting of the trap into which he had fallen, until the charms of the Company had been impressed on his mind. In the Cunard Line the "puff" appears in various disguises—all, however, winding up with the sentence in capital letters announcing it as "The Company which has never lost a man!"

We were, however, terribly cramped for space, officers as well as men. The ventilation found us out, too, as soon as the weather grew warm, hinting that the construction of vessels built for the Atlantic trade and cold weather was a little out of place in hot climates when crowded with soldiers.

Two companies were berthed on the "orlop deck," a subterranean-looking place which could only be gained by descending several ladders in a shaft which, for its black depth, might have led to a coal-mine. Daylight never reached this black-hole. By the dim light of the "bulls' eyes " could be seen the forms of men stripped to the waist, their bodies glistening with moisture, bending over the mess-tables, trying to read, or fingering dirty packs of cards. The tables were ranged in rows on either side, each accommodating twelve men. Against the ship's stern hung knapsacks, tin pots, straps, and odds and ends; from the deck protruded the hooks which supported the hammocks at night. The rifles stood in racks down the centre of the ship, —space already lumbered up with bales of spare blankets and hammocks for which no room could be found in the hold. At one end, under the shaft, was a hatchway, greasy with moisture and many feet. This was continually opened, and casks and other stores hauled into daylight by a gang of men, who still further diminished the light and air which struggled into this "infernal region." When it was cleared out on disembarkation, all the property lost during the voyage was unearthed from its recesses—rifles, bayonets, straps, bags, boots, clothing, all rusty or rotten from the damp and heat.

Thus early in the day our much-vaunted heroism began to receive some rude shocks.

At St Vincent, into which we put for coal, we experienced the first of a series of scares which came to us from that time until the close of the war—scares common to those whose hearts are bent on great things, and fear at every moment that they will not share in them.

As we rounded the Point, steamer after Steamer burst into sight. Here lay all the transports which had sailed for Africa before us. The *Russia*, Florence, City of Paris, Olympus, City of Venice, were in that quiet bay, with not a sign of moving on amongst them; and the idea quickly gained ground that the war was over without our assistance, and that telegrams detaining the troops had arrived.

The scare spread to the men; and it was curious to watch the crowd of faces peering towards the harbour, anxiously awaiting the pilot-boat which should put us out of our suspense. But no pilot came off; and it was not till we had steamed past the isolated rock which stands sentry over the entrance of the harbour, and had dropped anchor among the rest, that we learnt that the detention of the fleet was from want of coaling accommodation, and not from any bad news from England.

St Vincent, hitherto one of the quietest of the world's out-of-the-way nooks, enlivened only by a passing ship, woke up one fine morning to find herself the centre of the most extraordinary excitement. The water in the harbour was I dotted thickly with the huge iron hulls of transports, while fresh arrivals almost hourly kept sending up the flags at the tiny signal-station in a continued flutter. Fleets of boats filled with officers or men, all in uniform, were flying to and fro between the shipping and the long wooden pier, now crowded with people; the wire railway which conveyed sacks of coal from the depot to the lighters was everlastingly at work; the washerwomen in a crowd were pounding away at our linen at the stream outside the town; bugles were sounding, revolvers were cracking in continual practice, signal-flags were waving,—everywhere was life, bustle, and excitement.

The Praga da D. Luiz, a small square in the centre of the town by the sea, was thronged with visitors listening to a military band, sent ashore by one of the regiments, which discoursed waltzes and polkas, to the delight of the entire population, who gathered round twenty deep, dressed in gay-coloured clothes, many of the women executing dances of a somewhat florid character round the outer circle. The Hotel Luso-Brazileiro hard by was doing a roaring trade. Portuguese waiters were everywhere, flying with many gesticulations after liquids of sorts. The popping of corks was interminable, the Babel of languages quite indescribable.

"Waiter, beer!"

"Yes, my dear!"

"Waiter, brandy and soda!"

"At your service, my dear!"

Such were order and reply within that low, green-shuttered building.

The roofs of most of the houses are provided with a sliding opening, out of which the entire household can protrude their figures and look down upon the scene below,—a marvellously cheap way of getting a panorama of the surrounding world when required.

Above all shone a glorious sun, warming up the soldiers wistfully gazing at the shore they could not visit, with its delights of foreign damsels and cheap brandy. Poor fellows! they basked in the light and heat, forgetting the biting cold just parted from, and the close confinement down below.

But a Government comfortably at home, and ever mindful

of all things, had, as usual, forgotten one thing—the fact that a port adapted for the coaling of one steamer per week can hardly stand the strain put upon its resources when steamers requiring the same arrive by the dozen almost daily. Coals there were plenty, but boats were few, and men to work them fewer still; the? soldiers worked well on board when the coals, did come, but were unable to do more: so delay ensued, and nearly a week was lost, when telegrams urging our despatch with the utmost speed had been the motive power of the whole force.

Did the captain return on board, he was instantly pounced upon by a dozen anxious ones, with inquiries as to the number of lighters coming, and the probable time of departure. The officers of a battery of artillery on one of the transports, anxious to show an example to the men, lowered themselves into the coal-bunkers with the rest, and shovelled away at the descending coals with an utter disregard to fresh air or personal cleanliness.

Outside the harbour, as if infected with the general confusion, a whale spent an hour or more in jumping clean out of the water, and displaying his body and tail alternately for our gratification.

St Vincent left at last, the days passed in the usual routine-life common to troops on board ship. Of grumbling there was very little, of quarrels there were none-as one saturine man observed, "Thank Goodness, there are no women, so we have peace!" Courts-martial were frequent: the monotony told upon the men, and some of the higher spirits broke out and had to be suppressed. Pilfering small articles crept in, becoming a real nuisance, and had to be put down. Did a man clean his belts for parade, and lay them in the sun to dry, if he took his eyes off them for a moment, the chances were, his waist-belt or knapsack-straps had disappeared. A rifle, put away carefully cleaned in the rack, was gone the next morning, and the unarmed wretch appeared with fear and terror. Everything that a soldier has is marked with a number corresponding with that he himself is known by, so in theory it is easy to detect a man wearing another man's things; but practically, in a ship crowded with many more than a thousand souls, space is contracted, and to find out numbers on articles, all black and grimy more or less, is no easy matter. So many a pleasant morning was spent among the troops, fallen-in in long lines, swaying to and fro as the ship rolled, trying this somewhat unexciting game of finding out who was who by numbers.

The weather, too, on the "line," grew warmer than was pleasant, and the heat below was stifling. A stout captain found it especially so, and blew and puffed most vigorously—meals became distasteful to him, and night-time insupportable. Little Brown, who sat next to him at dinner, found his gigantic elbows somewhat in the way, and meekly gave in to superior rank by screwing his body into the smallest space possible. But heat, and the sufferings it entailed on our stout warrior, prevailed.

"Mr Brown," said a voice hoarse with anguish and much stretching, "I wish you would be good enough not to take up so much room."

Poor Brown, occupying inches to the other one's yards, retreated at the sound, till it looked as if he would vanish altogether; and for that day at least the gingerbread-nuts, and other delicacies beloved by boys, were untouched.

Another young officer had been provided by his anxious parents with a diary, magnificently got up in green leather and gold, in which he was to record his daily doings. For days he sat with the book before him, intent on the incidents of each hour, but finding none worthy of record. His devotion to the wishes of his parents, and to the diary, became a marked feature on board, and he was watched with much interest by the younger officers. At length he was seen to open the long-gazed-at volume, and seizing the pencil, make an entry. A rush was made at him instantly, and the book captured after a faint resistance; for the exertion of so much literary work had proved exhausting. So the book was taken from him, and the contents given out to the world at large: "March 20th —Saw a queer bird; query, condor?" For the rest of the campaign the youth was known as "The Queer Bird;" and little wonder! On another day we passed the homeward-bound Cape mail, but got no news from her of importance. Yet some bright spirits on board managed to extort a telegram from her as she steamed past us, which was carefully written out and put up in the place of honour in the saloon, amid some excitement among the juniors, who, pencil in hand, took it down, one after another, with touching faith and simplicity. The document thus inserted in many a diary and home-letter ran as follows: "*Nyanza* to *China*,—Kafir king prisoner, with first wife and son. Peace; but Boers continue troublesome. Reinforcements unnecessary. You will probably be sent to Fiji Islands."

These and other small amusements passed the days, weary enough as they were, till all our heads were turned towards the bows, where we were told the land was to be seen—a dim dark cloud over the eternal sea-line, growing darker every minute, till those who from the first said they saw it did see it with the rest of us, plainly now,—the great cliffs, frowning cold and grey, we were bound to—the mountains of South Africa—or, as we soon got to call it, the "Great Funkland!"

Chapter Three
Landfall—Africa

Simon's Town, where we put into for coal and other business, had set aside its usual sleepiness, and was all life and bustle.

At the anchorage lay the *City of Paris*, having just knocked a big hole in her bows, and therefore busy transferring the 21st, which she had brought out, to the square-built *Tamar*, with her heavy spars and cream-coloured hull—a good old troopship, known to most of us at one time or another.

Inside, again, were the *Olympus* and *Florence*, a fleet soon added to by the arrival of the *Russia*, thus transferring the excitement of St Vincent to this far-away spot. In the man-of-war anchorage lay the *Tenedos*, ordered home with a hole in her bottom, and the Active, flying the Commodore's pennant. Ashore were groups of officers intent on the latest news; squads of invalided soldiers, not considered strong enough for the front, and left behind in the Naval Hospital; naval officers cheery and full of spirits, all moving to and fro between the little club and the wharf over which the big South Atlantic waves kept dashing in a most uncomfortable way. Cape Town, twenty-four miles away, was equally excited by the landing of the Prince Imperial and the presence of more transports. Every one was abroad to see the Prince; ladies found shopping to do from morning till evening in the hopes of meeting him, and the theatre was decorated with tricolor flags, and a box retained for him under promise—so said the manager—of his presence: all to no purpose; the Prince stayed with the Governor, and did not move out at all.

The same afternoon some officers drove over to Cape Town to enjoy a few hours' relief from the constant companionship of the British soldier, soon to become apparently eternal, returning next day with the first instalment of the Great Funkland news. Men lately returned from Zululand had talked to them freely of the terrors of the place: defeat was a certainty— death indeed a mercy; tortures of the most appalling nature, described with a realistic force quite convincing, were the certain lot of those unfortunate enough to escape death. Isandlwana was an everyday occurrence in wars of this kind: the names of officers who had fallen there were quoted as instances of fresh horrors; their bodies had been recovered all but unrecognisable, owing to their treatment—or Zulu prisoners, previous to execution, had boasted of the tortures inflicted on Englishmen. The listeners were young and ready of belief, and the accounts of what they had heard cost nothing in the telling, and were detailed on board as the most cheerful news to be had.

The shadow of the Great Funkland was darkening over us already.

Indeed our stay at Simon's Bay was not the brightest part of our campaign. Our anxiety to get on, and to be in the middle of the war before too late, was a serious trouble. Our faith in our generals had not yet been shaken, and our great fear ever was lest the troops already in Natal should do the work without us. Anything was better than delay. Only let us be moving on, and we should be happy.

The news sent home of the peril imminent to the colony was still fresh in our minds. Hurried away at the shortest notice, we certainly felt that every delay was fraught with danger. What might not an hour bring out? Our advent in the threatened colony must be anxiously expected. Our landing would be the signal for the war to be brought to a conclusion one way or another. But delay followed delay; routine was everywhere — red-tape as rampant as at home. Cape Town, excited about the Prince and the tales of torture, found a far more burning question in the consideration whether it might not be called upon to contribute a share of the expenses. So to pass the time, and get away from our own thoughts, some of us drove over to Cape Town.

The road, such as it is, follows a portion of the shore of False Bay, in which again, in an indentation, lies Simon's Bay. It is a wild drive round the Bay, the road oftener than not following the sands, or mounting the cliff-side in an artificial cutting. Villages devoted to fishing are passed; a larger one, Kalk Bay, with some summer villas of the Cape people facing the sea — their bathing-machines the rocks, covered with seaweed, in front, as indeed we saw, without any attempt being made by the bathers to conceal the fact. At the head of the Bay stands a public-house, rejoicing in the name of *"Farmer Peck's,"* a picture of the *"Gentle Shepherd of Salisbury Plain,"* and a wonderful signboard with sentences on it in several languages, popularly said to be the work of a midshipman. It runs thus:—

"Multum in parvo, pro bono publico.
Entertainment for man and beast all of a row.
Lekker kost as much as you please.
Excellent beds without any fleas.
Nos patriam fugimus! now we are here.
Vivamus, let us live by selling Beer.
On donne a boire et a manger ici;
Come in and try it, whoever you be."

The inside, however, was as little tempting as the sign, two huge Dutch women presiding over a sloppy counter, across which we got some bad liquor at good prices.

After this, you leave the seashore and drive through a narrow and somewhat picturesque lane, with the mountains of the Cape on your left, until you arrive amidst the trees and dust which make up the greater part of Wyneberg, a pleasant suburb of the town.

To us the change of scene and life was enchantment. We lunched at a comfortable table laden with fresh fruit; we talked to young ladies and their mammas; less often with men in mufti, —just as we had done in England, as it seemed to us, weary months ago. Not a red-coat was to be seen; not a military phrase escaped any lips; even bad language, which had become second nature to our ears from the depths under our feet, was unheard. As for war, it was unknown, or ignored so totally that it would appear we had arrived as heralds of the millennium. It was indeed a new life to us. But a few hours before, we were surrounded by soldiers; arms and other deadly machines were our only ornaments; our books, pamphlets on the method of meeting an enemy in the field, and disposing of the slain after the encounter was over; our very thoughts centred in the work cut out for us. Ladies—their very name a thing of the past; homes all but forgotten in stern reality so imminent.

It was truly a case when those who had shouted, "*Morituri te salutant*," had come back alive once more out of the arena.

Cape Town itself, on the surface, appeared but little different from what it is in ordinary times. There were offices open, and placarded as places where volunteers for the war in Zululand could enrol themselves, and some of the enrolled ones about the streets, carbines in hand, going off to drill. The photograph-shops had some strange pictures of almost naked and quite hideous savages, labelled Zulus; but beyond this there was little else. As to Natal, it was a foreign country beyond the seas to the Cape Town people. Even its climate was unknown, and opinions were much divided between the wish, common to all colonists, to know all about everything, and the desire to ignore the place altogether. The only topic on which all were unanimous was the final cost of the war, and the shoulders of whom it would fall on. Not on those of Cape Town. Natal was a Crown colony—the Crown held it as its very own— and the Crown, of course, would pay the piper to the uttermost farthing. This, repeated on every occasion, with not the most pleasant hints thrown in that we and all other soldiers found the war greatly to our profit, grew quite monotonous, and sent us away from Cape Town but little impressed with the loyalty of its inhabitants.

Chapter Four
Preparing for the Campaign

After that, our last holiday, followed two days' buffeting with the waves of the Southern Ocean, and we cast anchor outside the "bar" at Durban. The town itself lies two miles inland, and is not visible from the anchorage, which is an open roadstead, much exposed to the south and east, whence come many of the gales prevalent in these latitudes. Across the whole bay, some two miles in length, stretches the bar, on which are only some five feet of water, compelling all except small vessels to lie outside. Inside is a magnificent bay, fringed with foliage, and bright and sparkling in the sunlight. Across the bar itself, and on the white sand of the beach beyond, the swells roll and break with a roar eternally. Opposite the beach the land stretches out into the sea in a high promontory called the "Bluff," steep and wooded, supporting a lighthouse on its extremity. General Funk, rampant in these days in the colony, had the assurance to tell us, with every appearance of sincerity, that a few days previously a Zulu was caught lurking near the lighthouse, and on being brought up and questioned, admitted that he was there by Cetewayo's orders, for the purpose of extinguishing the light, and thus make the English ships with the soldiers on board run ashore.

It was eight o'clock on the morning of the 2nd April when the ship anchored, and every one was eager to hear the news. Large clumsy tugs were plying about the shipping, *H.M.S. Shah* amongst the rest; and one of the former, with a post-captain standing on the paddle-box, was soon alongside. The news he brought was not comforting. Moriarty's death and the loss of his detachment on the Intombie river far in the north; the departure of the relief-column for Etshowe, about which nameless difficulties were predicted, — these were the principal items of news.

A more welcome sound came in the order to disembark at once, and soon the men began to fall in for the last time on the quarter-deck of the *China*. Captain and officers had done all in their power to lighten the monotony of the voyage; and on the previous day, the purser, in a set speech, had announced that the owners of the Cunard Company, Messrs Burns and M'lvor, wished to present the officers with the wine which they had drunk in no half-hearted way throughout the voyage. No one was sorry to leave the cramped confusion of the ship notwithstanding; and as soon as the accommodation-ladders were slung over the side, the men began swinging down them, passing their rifles first, and following themselves into the arms of a couple of sailors placed to catch them in the much-heaving tug.

"Catch a hoult of me legs, Barney darlint!" and appeals to "Holy Mother," or half the saints in the calendar, were frequent, and elicited shouts of laughter from those already down. It seemed as if the stream of struggling red-coated bodies would never cease. In vain the captain held up his hands and shouted that the boat was full—still down they came, tumbling and sprawling, till there was really no more squeezing room; and then it was only one company and the moiety of another that were out of the ship, and there were ten in all. The crew gave three cheers, and we pushed off, tossing and rolling quite as deep in the big swells as was, pleasant.

We passed some small vessels hard and fast on the bar, the water sucking in and out of the hatchways with a dismal sound. "Swish" came a spray, like a whip, right across our faces, and those who had waterproofs put them on; the men, crouching under the low bulwarks, grinned, and let off more jokes. Then came a huge roller, sending our boat down into the depths of the green water, and we were introduced to Durban bar. Another and another followed, broad, greasy swells, and with many lurches and splashing of salt spray, we got through into the quiet water inside.

Three ladies who had walked down to a sandy spit to watch our arrival, came in for a hearty British cheer, which they returned with much waving of parasols; and then we edged alongside the jetty, and were shunted ashore to make confusion more confused.

Here we first made acquaintance with the corduroy trousers worn as uniform under a regulation coat, common in the colony, not indeed from choice, but from necessity—a necessity, alas, we ourselves had to meet ere long! The landing officer—one great in his own way, though unknown to us—had a pair of these garments on underneath his befrogged and bemedalled coat, and came in for much curiosity in consequence.

The "Point," as our landing-place is named, was crowded with stores. Commissariat officers were hurrying about; streams of newly-arrived troops in bright clothes, and belts snow-white with pipeclay, met other streams of "fatigue parties" in damaged clothes and sprouting beards. The shore was piled high with cases on which the broad arrow sprawled, and the continually departing trains made but little diminution among them. Once, however, outside the Point and its confusion, and we were again marching along between rows of trees, with patches of grass and wild-flowers thickly strewn. Tiny wooden houses peeped out of the hedgerows; the greenest of turf stretched in front of them; wild-flowers were everywhere, and butterflies perched on the little mud-heaps which adorned the road here as in England.

Flag-staffs were abundant; every house had one, the object most noticeable to a stranger's eyes in their construction being that each one had been erected with a view to being higher than its neighbours. To an observant mind they suggest that the settlers in this part of the colony have passed a considerable portion of their lives at sea. Miniature flags fluttered from the tops of many of them, denoting the number of the transport just arrived.

Further on a school of small white children turned out and greeted us with a hearty cheer, as heartily responded to by the men. And it is worth recording that it was the only cheer which our countrymen gave us in the colony; they turned out to stare curiously at us, or rode alongside our column to cover us with dust, but welcome us with a cheer they did not. The colonists view the war in a light which appears strange to those in England, avowing that England got them into the mess, and that they look to her to get them out of it again. Hence they gave our troops no welcome after their long journey out to help them. The local papers teemed with letters and articles ventilating this side of the question, and might have gained a part of what they wished had not the colonists been so eager about the apportioning of Zululand after the war.

"My brave young man," said a fellow-passenger in the train to me at that time, "you'll get 20,000 acres of it, of course, as soon as ever that old cuss Cetewayo is kicked out."

This was the ruling sentiment; and much anger and disappointment were caused by the telegram which stated that England would make her own terms with the Zulus, which would be especially directed against annexation, while the question of the share in the expenses of the war would be settled hereafter.

Covered vans full of people passed each other and us on the road, and were labelled "omnibus;" past some stores, where Huntley & Palmer and Morton were well represented, by the side of the inevitable russet-brown corduroy trousers and flapping wideawakes, and we turned out of West Street, the principal thoroughfare of Durban, crossed the railway, and reached our camping-ground quite ready for dinner—of which, however, there was little chance.

We were on a low-lying strip of grass, some two miles in length, and half that width, popularly supposed to swarm with ticks, and so to be unfit for cattle, though good enough for soldiers. One side is enclosed by a high bank, sandy and tree-grown, beyond which is the sea; on the other lies "the Berea," a hog-backed ridge, prettily covered with trees, from out of which peep the picturesque country villas of the better class in Durban.

The ground we were on, besides the ticks, which were a real and feeling annoyance, has its own history. Here, in 1841, lay the English, beleaguered by the Boers, whom we had followed into this country, then their own. Fighting ensued, as a matter of course; Durban was retaken by the Dutch; its garrison reduced to eating their own boots in a *"laager"* outside the town, built on the site of our present camp; and total extinction imminent, till one Dick King swam with two horses across the bay at night, passing the sleepy Dutch sentries in safety, and riding into King William's Town, many miles distant, for succour.

Opposite our camp four Gatling guns were posted, with their artillerymen about them, all waiting for horses to take them to the front. Through the centre of the tents passed a road, then a moving scene of men and carts. One waggon in particular passed a hundred times a-day. It was painted in bright colours, and was drawn by a team of sixteen mules, which ambled along nimbly to the persuasions of a long whip, which a burly Kafir, standing in front on the load, handled like a fishing-rod. It was our introduction to mule-waggons; from henceforth our lives were to be passed in their continual company.

Queerly dressed volunteers swaggered past, distinguished by a bit of red rag wound round their hats, or even round their heads, if they were "off-coloured" and dispensed with such luxuries. Their particular swagger was to stick a riding-whip in their boots. As a rule, they had at least a pint of bloodshed in each eye, with an unmistakable preference for drink, which had in many cases militated against their success in other walks of life.

Everywhere was bustle, noise, and confusion. The sleepy little town had woke up to find itself famous. Until the war developed, its inhabitants divided their time between selling Hollands gin and slop-clothes, dining at one of the two clubs, which they have established, and doing an occasional deal in ponies. Then came Isandlwana and panic. A defence committee was formed, barricades erected, the post-office and market-house pierced with loop-holes and surrounded with sandbags, the Point cut off by a stout palisade of huge timbers and sheet-iron. Country people flocked into the *"laager,"* as any temporary enclosed spot was called, and every one looked for the worst, and hoped for the aid which had been asked for with such urgency from England. Nor was the panic to be laughed at. The Zulus had proved themselves a terrible foe; murder and fire were their only arguments; in a few hours they could overrun the colony, and that was defenceless.

Two months thus passed—months to be remembered with sorrow and bitterness; and on a given day the *Pretoria* steamed into the harbour with the 91st, the first of the long-expected reinforcements, followed quickly by the 60th Rifles. The fine old soldiers of the 57th had already arrived from Ceylon; Mauritius and St Helena had both sent their all. A few days later the *Tamar* put ashore the 21st; the *China* brought the 94th; the *Russia* the 58th. Artillery and Engineers filled up the intervals. The great horses which the Army Service Corps landed were special objects of admiration among people who looked to purchasing bargains when the war was over. Lastly came in the great four-masted steamers of the National Line, with the much-believed-in cavalry. The King's Dragoon Guards and 17th Lancers landed their horses as bright and well as if-they had not been a day from Aldershot, and the people for once cheered them,—the horses, not the men—so it was said at the time.

So Durban cheered and woke up. The "scare" was over; merchants made money faster than their best dreams ever hoped for; the clubs made all military men members, to the discomfort of their own, who were elbowed out of doors, and from their own particular places, by the eager, hungry new-comers; ponies went up to fabulous prices; every one had a wonder in horse-flesh to sell; in the rare event of one not being a seller, he had a friend, or more, ready to oblige. Things went on swimmingly, and telegrams from the front with accounts of further fighting only served to strengthen the hope that the war might last for ever.

At the club "shandy-gaff" is a popular drink. If you wish for champagne, "dry Monopole" is the only brand admitted into society in Natal. After a meal, small bits of paper are handed round, on which you write what you have had; and the custom obtains all over the colony. The members appeared to have tried other modes of life previous to their present occupations: most of them are retired something or other; nearly all have been in fights somewhere with natives, so the conversation round the table is warlike. Lord Chelmsford came in for praise and blame pretty equally. The volunteers, as was only natural, had done great things. About the future of the war, opinions were mixed. We should walk through Zululand like a hot knife through butter; nothing is easier if we make our waggons into a *laager* every night, and drive right through. As a matter of fact, the warrior who made so light of the Zulus was suspected of having sold them many guns; he was, besides, much too fat to move far from the club, so his assertions were not likely to be tested personally. Another shook his head, and prophesied that Cetewayo would let us into the country, and then burn the grass. On our still looking for further details, it was explained that when the grass is burnt we might consider ourselves as dead men, the oxen would die, and—there you are.

But whatever the hopes or fears of our friends, all were unanimous in the wish that we should exterminate the Zulu nation. Nothing else but total annihilation would satisfy their thirst for vengeance, and enable them to annex the country. The conversation was thus rather bloodthirsty, and it was a relief to turn to sixpenny whist and another glass of shandy-gaff.

But though panic had subsided, General Funk was abroad, and knocking at many hearts, even in so distant a spot as Durban.

The defences at the Point and post-office were kept in a state of readiness; arms were in every house; drunken natives caught about the camp were invariably accused of being Zulu spies, and collected large crowds interested in glimpses of the enemy, even when in liquor.

"And do you say that you do not post pickets at night round your camp?" said one colonist. "Why, the Zulus can be here in sixteen hours, and that wood over there can hold 20,000 men and you not see one of them."

Nor were our own people a bit better. One of the first orders we received was to dye our white helmets the colour of the ground, so as to afford no marks to the Zulu sharpshooters. Elephant-hunters, we heard from another source, were to be particularly shunned on account of their deadly aim; while from a semi-official intimation we were advised to assimilate our dress as much as possible with that of the men, the Zulus knowing accurately the number of officers in each corps, and having ten *Indunas* or chiefs told off for every officer in each battle, whose orders were to make straight for the officers, and sacrifice their lives rather than let us escape. So at the outset we felt that the odds were ten to one against each of us.

One excellent rule was published, though it was grumbled at for the time. The campaign was to be a teetotal one. Liquor was to be as strictly excluded as poison. Thus carriage was saved— something more than the mere expense of waggons — and the men were at all times ready to fight with their wits about them. The officers, to their credit be it said, fell in with the rule almost to a man, not quite turning into total abstainers, but cutting and trimming manfully, being careful that what bottles were produced were only opened in private, and not in view of the men.

A code of general rules was issued to all of us, many of them of the highest importance, as indeed the first in the book told at a glance:—

"*When troops take the field, regulations which are applicable to station-work and peacetime must not be considered as binding, should the enforcement of them tend to increase instead of diminish difficulties.*"

Another rule which we read with unconcern, through ignorance, was hereafter the greatest hardship we endured. It said: "*The troops will invariably turn out under arms at least two hours before sunrise, and silently occupy their respective alarm-posts. They will similarly again fall in every evening at the first post at tattoo.*" Tattoo, we were told a little further on, "*will be at 8 P.M., after which lights must be extinguished, and the whole camp, without exception, remain perfectly quiet until the next morning.*"

32

Alas! how well we soon got to know those dark, quiet nights, with that awfully early rouse, cold, sleepy, and miserable. Another excellent paragraph ordered that companies were to be kept intact, and not broken up; sentries were to be posted, too, in groups of four, so that they might derive moral support from their comrades; and at the end of a march the officers were enjoined to examine the men's feet in search of blisters, when the sufferer was at once to be sent to a doctor. Lastly, blacking was to be disregarded for grease or "dubbing," and cotton shirts for flannel. We learnt in the sick regulations still further, that a couple of threads of worsted should be drawn through a blister. So even the most insignificant details were taken into account. Meanwhile came in the news of the battles of Ginginhlovu and Kambula—the first successes we had had, and hailed accordingly; and we having been appointed to the 2d Division, under Major-General Newdigate, received the order for the front.

Now began the repacking and selection of our own kits, which had to be reduced to the regulation forty pounds—little enough to last for a probable six, and, as it turned out, nearly twelve, months' campaign, in a climate varying between frost at night and semi-tropical heat by day. Now the outfitters came in for a share of well-earned abuse, by reason of the useless and really expensive articles declared indispensable at home, to be abroad rudely got rid of. An india-rubber bed with a pair of bellows to inflate it, a hammock, slung delicately between neat poles, with a canvas awning over the whole; suits of "South African" mufti, white shirts, table-cloths, looking-glasses, and a hundred other suchlike, were all put on one side with a lingering look of regret, and still the forty-pounds were exceeded. So out went the extra flannel shirts, patent tubs, brushes and combs, slippers, and so on, until the black valise, looking very empty, just turned the scale, and was allowed to pass.

On the way out the chances of the war had been a never-failing source of discussion, and it was generally agreed that ten days after landing we should find ourselves on the Tugela, face to face with the Zulus. After that, all must be uncertain—depending, as it would do, on the enemy's own movements; but within the month we all fondly hoped the decisive battle would be fought. Yet here we were, after nearly a week wasted in Durban, sent off to a station in the north of Natal, some twenty days distant, which, when arrived at, left us little nearer the Zulus than we were to-day. Thus our month was already a delusion.

Chapter Five
Marching into the Country

From Durban the rail took us some twenty miles to Botha's Hill, the men riding in cattle-trucks, the officers in second-class carriages, as the "Natal Government Railways" are still in embryo, and not prepared for much extra traffic. On the line itself curves and steep gradients are the rule, and the rise for the first few miles is very marked. The low country lying round the coast is covered with "bush," as woods are called in Natal; open park-like spaces, dotted with tree-clumps, break the monotony; gorges, impassable through a tangle of semi-tropical vegetation, run down from the sides of the frequent mountains, and are named "*kloofs*," after the old Dutch word. Elephants not so many years past disported in these. Bamboos, ever graceful, feather the crests of the ridge on either side. Plantains flap their broad leaves in the sheltered nooks. The flat-topped mimosa-bush, white with long thorns, is almost everywhere. Patches of Indian corn, the colonial "mealies," are plentiful. Houses alone are wanting: a clump of blue gum-trees is a sign that one is near; hardly a farm in Natal is without this elegant and, rapid-growing stranger. Beyond the coast, trees are rare, almost unknown, and some shade is necessary, so the farmer is driven to plant a circle round his house, thus obtaining firewood and shelter together.

Higher up, the bush gives way to grasslands, the ordinary feature of landscape in the colony. The grass grows tall and rank, green in spring, yellow in summer, when it is burned, for the double purpose of fertilising the ground and destroying the ticks. Were this last precaution not taken, the ticks would increase so enormously as to render cattle impossible. For the same reason hay cannot be made. It is said with some truth that on the end of every grass stalk is a tick, waiting to spring on the first living thing passing by. As it is, the poor oxen are often a mass of hideous, leaden-coloured lumps, dependent from their flanks; and it is a wise precaution, before going to bed, to examine one's own shins, as it is highly probable that some of the species have effected a lodgment during the day. Pulling is of little use —the head breaks off and forms a sore; a drop of carbolic oil, and the insect drops out.

The archdeacon, a fine specimen of an English clergyman, accompanied us in the train, and was full of chatty information.

This was the plantain-tree, that a pine-apple; from the tall tree came cotton, the short one produced ginger; and a hundred other bits of information somewhat stale to a regiment from India. At Pinetown, about half way, destined to become a big overgrown depot for our troops, our friend insisted on sending for sherry and sandwiches from the hotel hard by, to which, after some demur, we did ample justice. In the end, the kind-hearted old parson accompanied us on the road for some miles, walking beside the column cheerily enough, and parting from us with an affectionate blessing on the heads of "his brave boys,—may God bless and keep you!"

Leaving the train at the top of the range, a glorious view opened out,—the land a vast sheet of green, crumpled up like a piece of stiff paper retaining the creases; the slopes dotted with cattle and the mushroom-like *kraals* of the Kafirs; the *kloofs* richly wooded; in the centre a flat-topped mountain, its upper sides scarped with a wall of naked rock, its edge sharp and knife-like, the forerunner of many such, which are the characteristic form of high land in Upper Natal and Zululand. Beyond this mountain, again, is a chaos of flat-topped ranges, beneath, which flows the Lower Tugela. In the far distance lies the sea, grey and hazy, the shipping at Durban looking like dots upon it.

What few natives we met were innocent of clothing, save the "mouche" of fur in front and behind, and not unlike a lady's "bustle." They were fine-looking men, grinning good-naturedly, and holding up one hand above the shoulder as they salute us with the usual formula, "*Inkos*"—chief.

At the actual summit was a group, perched evidently in

36

expectation of our coming; and as we appeared, the whole set up a wild imitation of a cheer, crying out, "Oolay, Johnnie! Go cut dam Zulu throat!" suiting the words with an exact pantomimic representation of the deed.

Of course the soldiers were delighted, and gave them a cheer in return, the Johnnies in their friendliness shouting after them—"You come back, Johnnie! yes, you come back, I say, —oolay!"

The road wound round the great swells of grass-land like a serpent, and the red line of men, stretched out to a considerable length between advance and rear guards, looked picturesque enough. The pretty white helmets of Aldershot had disappeared; the spikes, so martial-looking there, had gone, with every vestige of pipeclay washed out of the belts: but the men stepped along cheerily, whistling or singing popular airs, till the dust got into their throats, and there was a rush at the first halting-place to fill their water-bottles. The streams, tempting at a distance, proved to be dried up; so those who made for them had their climb for nothing. The more knowing ones gave a trifle of tobacco to a Kafir, and he soon brought back a supply of the hot muddy liquid which in the colony does duty for water.

It was a weary tramp that first night, our feet fresh to the road, our muscles relaxed by the confinement of shipboard, and the men unused to pitching their tents, especially in the dark. At length our own was up, and turned out a tight fit for three to live, eat, and sleep in continually. Then came difficulties about our dinner. Some lean beef had been served out to us, water was pretty handy, wood was also provided, and we had a most neat Aldershot canteen; and that, with a pound of heavy bread and our soldier-servants, represented our first camp-dinner. Well, the beef was cut into bits and boiled quickly, so as to be ready soon, and sure enough, appeared in hard lumps floating in greasy water, utterly unpalatable, but necessary to existence. So we ate, and went to bed, lying in a blanket on the ground, which was harder than we expected, it is true; but then it was a campaign, and you can't get used to hardships soon enough.

Maritzburg—or, as most colonists delight in calling it,

Maratsburg, or P.M. Burg—lies at one end of a broad, elevated valley, on the banks of a tolerably good river, its pools prettily shaded with willows, and fringed with a setting of wild-flowers. The houses, mostly wooden cottages of one storey, with gabled roof, peep out of a grove of blue gum-trees, making it green and pleasant to the eye. Outside the town the country is bare enough: not a tree is to be seen except those round houses; streams flowing on muddy bottoms cross the road, and give rise to fearfully long delays in the traffic. Behind the town is a range of hills without a single gap, and up this travellers further into the country must climb. There is no escape.

It was across this lower plain that we marched, weary and dry-throated. The sun beat down with almost tropical fierceness, and the dust rose in white impalpable clouds. To do honour to the chief town in the colony, we were taken round through the main street, instead of marching direct on our camping-ground. Crowds of well-dressed townspeople turned out to see us, and in their honour our half-dozen drummer-boys moistened their lips sufficiently to play a bugle-march at the head of the column. But no answering cheer met our poor efforts at military pomp, no friendly hand put out even a bucket of water to wet the soldiers' lips. Dry and dusty, they marched to the camp-ground above Fort Napier, and threw themselves on the ground quite tired out;

Maritzburg was alive with uniforms. Volunteers of every description sauntered up and down the pavements, giving a dim idea that their services in the Zulu war would begin and end in that peaceful town. Not that it was considered worthy of that epithet by the inhabitants. On the contrary, General Funk had pointed it out as the point to which danger and attack were chiefly directed. Nearly every house showed signs of preparation for the enemy—windows planked up, garden-railings boarded, openings closed with galvanised iron; everywhere were loop-holes and blank defensible walls.

The principal street was disfigured by an ugly structure of iron and timber, enclosing some hundred yards or more, including a church and many shops; while close to it stood the handsome

Parliament House and post-office, sadly mutilated with loop-holes and sand-bag parapets. Until lately, this *laager*, and the town generally, was filled with fugitives from the country; prices went up in consequence, and had not recovered. Eggs fetched 4s. a dozen, oranges were 3d. each, cucumbers were 9d., butter almost unprocurable.

Every one, however, can manage some sort of horse-flesh, and having done so, keep their possession, whenever possible, at full gallop. Young ladies ride about unescorted, and do their shopping in the saddle.

Some six miles outside I happened to put up for a day with a farmer whose history, as told by himself, may be relied on as a fair type of what can be done in the colony by an industrious man.

"Twenty-seven years ago," said my friend, "a lot of us made up our minds to leave Yorkshire and come out here. The colony was just started, and a good deal was said about it in the papers. We were to do without one of those agents who only fleece emigrants, and so we took a ship in Hull for the colony; there were some 250 of us on board. I had my wife, mother, and two brothers, besides a hundred golden sovereigns in my belt. They kept us nearly two months in Hull, but we got away at last, and landed in safety. Then we came up here and settled at York (Natal) all together. But we found that there were too many of us, so we separated. That was seven-and-twenty years ago. Now I've ten children. One son has a farm all his own, of 800 acres, and keeps himself. Another is employed by Government as a conductor in the war. The third is at school. The seven girls and my old woman you have seen here.

"This farm is 1500 acres, all my own, and I refused two years ago three pounds an acre for it. I've got two other ones besides, nearly as much again. I've got a steam-engine to crush the mealies, and two waggons worth £400 apiece. There was never a year I did not clear £100; but then I never speculated in land, and I keep clear of the drink."

Probably the secret of success lay in this last short paragraph.

On leaving Maritzburg, our way lay over the range already spoken of, and to the right of the main road. Ours was to be the shorter road by Greytown, much nearer the Zulu border, and thus thought too unsafe for traffic until assured by our presence. Even Lord Chelmsford and his staff avoided it, and used the main road in preference, after Isandlwana, General Funk being then in full swing.

"Your guns will go off, won't they, now they have sent you along that dreadful road?" said a fond old lady to us the night before we left Maritzburg—showing that the last-named General had not yet vacated his command.

Chapter Six
Marching through Natal

Natal has been described as a country of rivers without water, flowers without scent, birds without song, and where every dog is called "*Foot-sack*" (Dutch, be off), and runs away when you call him ; and the description may be taken generally as accurate. But as the exception proves the rule, so do the falls of the Umgeni river, some miles north of Maritzburg, stand out in relief as a beautiful contrast to the general character of the water-courses.

A broad, still river, flowing through a valley turfed with the greenest grass, often up to a man's shoulders, sometimes shooting up in waving patches 12 feet high; presently comes a step some 50 feet in height, and the silent river is broken into a series of cascades, the spray from which paints a rainbow against the morning sun. The stream opens out like a funnel; the cascades divided by pillars of basalt, tipped with bushes, from whose branches the weaver-birds have hung their nests.

There are eleven separate falls, in the shape of a horse-shoe, about 300 yards in length. Beyond this are jets of water tumbling into foam for nearly twice that distance.

The roar of the water in that vast plain is heard long before the falls are seen, and is as difficult to understand as it is unexpected. Across the boiling pool into which the river tumbles is a thicket of rank grass, with fallen boulders, wet with spray, and overgrown, with clematis and other climbing-plants; tall grasses nod and feather in the wind; grasshoppers, with butterfly wings, are springing everywhere. On the summit of a basalt column mid-stream a pair of hoodie-crows had built a nest, six feet high, and were perching on it, croaking loudly.

There is a canteen, as wayside inns are called in the colony; near the falls, where breakfast can be had, and beer at half-a-crown a bottle. The price of beer is as good as a set of milestones in Natal. From Durban upwards it was 2s. a bottle; at Maritzburg the price rose to 2s. 6d.; beyond Greytown you paid 3s.; beyond the Tugela it rose to 3s. 6d.; at Dundee, where the central column was formed, you paid 6d. more, and were lucky if you could get it at the price; while at Utrecht, those who drank beer paid 7s. 6d. a bottle.

English money obtains throughout the colony, with a notable abundance of half-crowns. Florins are called "Scotchman," the accent being on the a, the tradition being that they were introduced in considerable numbers by a North Briton, and passed off on the Kafirs as the well-known half-crowns. The simplest Kafir now understands the difference. Threepennies and fourpennies pass as the same coin; to coppers there is a decided objection.

When a man up-country makes money, he gets a friend going down to carry the sovereigns to Maritzburg or Durban; there are no banks elsewhere, and no other way of remitting, consequently cheques are taken with a facility which would be interesting to many whose paper nearer home is apt to be looked at with suspicion.

Near Greytown we came across a herd of hartebeests. They are under protection by Government, forming a charming addition to the otherwise inanimate plain. The Umvoti cuts across the country here—here narrow, there widening into broad reaches, where the oxen stand knee-deep. Immediately beyond it rises the mountain-range, supporting the plateau of the northern portion of Natal. The plains about us are covered with the conical mud-heaps of white ants. These are as hard as brick, and contain countless chambers and galleries. Under many of them a hole has been excavated by the ant-bear— an animal seldom seen—which digs very rapidly, and, getting underneath the nest, feeds at its leisure. Not long before the war the hounds of the 24th ran into one near Cape Town, and after worrying it for some time, being whipped off, the animal was taken up with hardly a scratch on its tough hide.

Cut off as we were now from the outer world, we felt the want of news most acutely.

Kambula had just been fought and Etshowe relieved when we left Durban, and the most important results might be expected. We were daily moving towards the scene of action; Zululand was now but a short distance in front; we knew that the regiment was destined to take part in the operations against Ulundi,— yet we were here now as utterly uninformed of the course of events as were the Zulus themselves. For all we knew to the contrary, the war might have been concluded; or more probably still, the Zulu nation might even now be marching into Natal. However, there was no help for it but to do as we had been told, and continue our march.

Greytown itself contains a few houses surrounded by blue gums. The inhabitants are mostly Dutch, and were, when we arrived, largely increased by the people of the district, who had made a camp between their waggons in a most primitive way. Outside, tiny Dutch dolls, with flat faces, were tumbling seriously; inside, the Vrow was cooking bacon for the rough -bearded man in boots and red-cord breeches, who was the husband, and a fair type of the Boer.

An old lady keeps a boarding-house in the town, and thither all the English on their travels who wish for dinner have to go. It is a tumble-down place; oleanders and pomegranates flower in the garden; tall gum-trees shade it from the sun; and a couple of Kafir boys sweep out the veranda, dancing in slow time to their own accompaniment. Some stir was caused by a swarm of bees which had taken possession of a portmanteau belonging to one of us. They completely filled it; and the dilemma of the owner, as he viewed the intrusion from a distance, was most amusing. Greytown, as a matter of course, had its *laager*. This was an enclosure surrounded by a wall some 10 feet high. Inside was a house containing munitions of war; round the wall ran a *banquette* for the men to stand upon; the ground was strewn with more warlike materials. Admittance was by a door strongly barred. Outside ran a ditch. Beyond this was the camp of some infantry, also strongly fortified. A large house in the vicinity had been pulled down by the troops, as commanding the post, at a cost to Government estimated by the owners at £10,000. This stupendous work had already been introduced to the public in England through the columns of an illustrated paper.

After Greytown, we climbed the hills we had seen when on the other side of the Umvoti. Flat-topped, and terraced with steps of naked rock, the range rises towards the north. The rise is abrupt, and the change in climate most decided. The summit was enveloped in clouds, and our clothes were saturated; everything was damp and chilly. An hour later the men were basking in the warmest sunshine at Burrop's.

Burrop is a man, and he gives his name to the spot his cottage occupies. Near him is Botha, also down on the map. Both are small farmers, the latter being the proprietor of the former. Burrop, in addition, sells liquor and keeps a canteen. Burrop was an Eton man. He came out to the colony years ago in a high position under Government, from which he has gradually descended, till he owns a small cabin on a mountain, a patch of mealies, and a cupboard full of "square-face" and bottled beer. If you breakfast at Burrop's, your tea will be poured out by his daughter, a most charming young lady, looking very much out of place, and acknowledged as the belle of Umvoti—so the district is called. From Burrop's a grand view across the valley of the Mooi river is obtained. On the right, Mount Allard raises its flat top to 5000 feet above the sea, just hiding the mountains of Zululand and the line of the Tugela; below, the entire valley for many miles is a jumble of broken ground covered with mimosa-bushes.

This belt of country is known as "The Thorns," and is much dreaded. In width it extends across the Tugela and Mooi rivers for some thirty miles, stretching across the whole colony as far, and beyond Colenso and Escourt, fifty miles west. Water is scarce; grass there is none; the heat is intense; and the loose, friable soil rolls away from under every step. The bushes are armed with thorns, from an inch to four inches long, which bristle horribly from every twig; weird cactus, euphorbias, and aloes, spined and horrent, supported by a stem of dead leaves, spiked even in death, are scattered about. As they range about six feet high, and are much the size of a native's body, they were constantly

44

mistaken for lines of advancing Zulus, causing a constant call for field-glasses and telescopes. Flowers had disappeared; rocks, baked clay, and gullies torn and rent by thunderstorms, were on every side. The gullies, under the name of donga, we had cause to remember as we advanced. Skeletons of oxen, which had fallen as they went, were scattered along the road. The valley was shut in by flat-topped mountains, seamed with shelves of naked rock. The water-courses were dry sand, and the men plodded along rather wearily, their empty water-bottles rattling by their sides. Through the centre runs the Mooi river—at the place where we crossed it, a good, swift-flowing stream. Then came a steep climb, and the road topped a pass over a long hill-range, and below us lay the Tugela, glistening in the sunlight.

The name was historic; and from the anxious looks cast upon it, one would think that the whole Zulu army was expected to be seen upon its banks. Instead, we gazed upon a wilderness of greenery: hills and valley were alike clothed in the same beautiful mantle. The roadside was a carpet spangled with flowers of bright hues,—the blue stems of the castor-oil bush, with its vine-shaped leaves and prickly fruit; mauve-coloured salvias, in graceful masses; purple ipomseas, climbing over everything; white jasmine—scentless, alas! —mingled its tendrils with convolvuli of every size and colour; zinnias blazed in scarlet and orange,—all contributing to the effect.

The men quickened their step, marching merrily down the steep incline to the notes of a concertina, which gave out popular tunes, with variations not to be found in the music-books.

"Play on the box, Mister Halligan!" shouted a voice from the rear to the man who was carrying it; and the small joke took them down a mile or more. How the oxen brought the waggons down that incline was a puzzle to us, then unused to the feats of climbing common to those animals. It was just a succession of muddy hollows, separated by intervals, over which the waggons slid gaily down table-rocks at every angle with the horizon. This was varied by piles of loose stones, water-courses, with banks to get down and up like the roof of a house, and ruts a foot or more deep. The Government engineer who planned and cut that road was freely commented on during the march.

A party of native scouts was in front of the column, armed with many assegais and shields— formidable to look at, but at heart ready to bolt at the first; rustle in the bushes. Presumably to give us due warning of the approach of the Zulus, these scouts kept some five yards ahead of the sergeant-major at the head of the line, and appeared much too busy dividing the scraps of food they had picked up to keep a look-out, except upon one another. They were one of the many impostures then believed in.

Just as we reached the river, a shot was heard close to us among the bushes, which might have been the Zulus, but was only directed against an ox, that came staggering across, falling dead to a second shot—the primitive mode of butchering in the colony, but nevertheless meaning dinner.

The Tugela is a fine river, broad, and in parts deep, and was no doubt an excellent protection against the Zulus, who, cat-like, do not care too much about wetting their feet.

Before this, as it was, we had our first "scare." A few natives came into camp with the news that they had seen the Zulus crossing the river some ten miles distant. All was at once hurry and bustle: men were recalled by the bugles, ammunition was got ready—each man, by the way, carried seventy rounds at his waist—and the order to "form *laager*" was issued. No one thought of asking for details of the Zulu advance,—how many they were? armed or unarmed? Zulus or Kafirs? The scare was a novelty to us, and much too delightful to be made light of,—it might end in a fight; it must give us a little shooting: at last we were going to meet the enemy!

But it was our first *laager*, and we were very raw. The waggons were heavy to drag about; and nothing would content us till every one was placed in the most approved fashion. Each waggon fitted in exactly to the one next to it, so that not a hole was left through which a Zulu could crawl; the oxen were tied down securely, unable to "bolt" during the firing, and were nearly strangled in their efforts to escape; while, to crown it all, the men, formed in two beautiful lines, which stretched far across the road into the bushes beyond, moved in at the sound of the bugle in unbroken ranks, getting into their allotted places with as much order and regularity as do the child-soldiers in the plays at home. The only thing to mar the excellence of, our scheme was the time it took to complete—nearly two hours—while the Zulus could have been on us in less than half that period. It was, besides, labour thrown away, as we might have known all along, had not General Funk taught us some lessons—the Kafirs who had invented the news saying, a little later, that the Zulus crossing were all friends, numbering just a dozen.

The usual *laager* is formed by drawing each waggon as it arrives into a ring or square previously marked? out at the corners, either allowing them to lap over one another, when an "echelon" is formed, or running the "*dessel-booni*," or pole, of each under the waggon in front. Thus a wall of them surrounds an open space. A waggon is left out at one place for an opening, to be filled in when required by a spare one, water-carts, and so on. The waggon-wheels may be lashed together, and the spaces between them filled in with thorns. With us, this space was banked up with earth; or, latterly, a shelter-trench was dug round the whole circumference at some fifteen feet distance, so as to form the first line of defence, the line of waggons being the second. The loads can, further, be piled along the outer side of the waggons, so as to form a parapet from which the men, lying down, can fire with security. In large *laagers* the oxen are tethered inside, the men's tents being outside. A man is told off to each as the poleman — his duty being, on an alarm, to pull out the tent-pole, when the tent falls, and forms an obstacle to an advance, while he runs inside with the pole, in readiness to produce it when the tent is again to be put up.

The Cape waggon is a huge machine double the size of that in use in England. The body is low, the hind wheels as large again as the fore ones, and it is altogether roughly made to withstand rough usage on roads unworthy of the name. Behind,- it is furnished with a tilt, under which the travellers sleep, and is entirely innocent of springs.

Sixteen oxen are the usual team, but eighteen and twenty are often seen. These are yoked in spans of two, the yoke's heavy beams connected by a wire-rope or chain.

A waggon in South Africa is another term for capital invested. Every person of the smallest importance has one or more, their cost varying, with a team, from £300 to £400. During the war the price of oxen in the colony had nearly doubled, and transport or locomotion thus became almost unattainable.

A team of oxen is a separate body seldom changed, and each ox knows his own place in the team. The drivers and *"foreloopers"* or leaders, are clever fellows in managing their teams; but let a white man go near, and a kick, a snort, or a poke from horns awkwardly long and sharp will reward him. The yoke-chain, or *"trek tow,"* is laid on the ground during the *"outspan;"* and when it is required to *"inspan,"* the team is driven towards it, when each ox takes up his place on either side of the chain, facing inwards.

The heads of each span are then coupled together with *"reims,"* or strips of raw, dry hide; and when all are tied together, they are pushed under the yokes, and fastened in with a peg called a *"yokeskey",* and the waggon is ready. The driver stands balancing himself on the top, and flourishing an enormously long whip; the forelooper pulls at the reim of the foremost span; a desperate volley of shrieks, yells, and hideous guttural cries, accompanied by cracks of the whip as loud as musket-shots, succeeds, and the huge affair is in motion. If required to stop, the men set up a chorus of whistling, and the oxen obey.

Chapter Seven
Into Zululand

Fort Bengough was a square enclosure on an isolated hill overlooking the green valley of Umsinga. It was constructed early in the war by the officer whose name it bears. The valley itself, which falls down to the Buffalo on the east, and so is within easy reach of the Zulus, had been the scene of several scares, in one of which some of our native troops from the fort were shot down by our own men in mistake for the enemy.

The regiment of Natal Native Contingent, to which they belonged, marched out as we arrived, to do us honour with their war-dance.

Imagine seven hundred naked savages in companies of one hundred each; their only clothing the tiny kilt of fur; perhaps a plume of ostrich-feathers on their head, or a strip of leopard-skin round the forehead. Many dress their hair in strange fashions — divided like waves of the sea, twisted into points, or peaked into a central ridge, like a cock's comb. All carry an oval shield of black and white cowhide, four assegais, and a *knob-kirri*; some few have muskets. Amongst them stalk giants, their bodies glistening with oil, full seven feet high, true sons of Anak, magnificently built and proportioned. Many more are upwards of six feet in stature, and are models of symmetry and savage grace.

Each company advances brandishing shields and assegais aloft to some native tune, slow time admirably kept, its chant being continually varied by deep gutturals, hisses, grunts, and shouts, all uttered in the most perfect time. Their eyes roll, and they give out the war-song with startling energy and ferocity as they pass. Every here and there a warrior dashes out of the ranks, and goes through in pantomime the pursuit, defeat, and ultimate slaughter of an imaginary foe—accompanying the performance by leaps, tumbles, crawlings, and the most hideous grimaces; his

49

fellows in the ranks greeting him with a wild chorus of shrieks, and cries of encouragement and admiration; now whistling or giving out the deep guttural "*ouf-oom-squish*;" now bursting out, yelping like a pack of dogs; occasionally, when excited by some warrior more grotesque than usual, rushing out to imitate him, three and four at a time.

One chief, of huge proportions, had managed to hoist himself on to a horse—the animal looking mean under the weight he carried, which was indeed every inch the noble savage.

At daybreak, when we marched, our allies headed us off and lined the road, as much to their own delight as to that of our soldiers, who, having picked up some bits of the native air, greeted them with the quaint "*ouf-oom-squish*;" eliciting in return grins innumerable, and the universal "Ha, ha, Johnnie!"

The natives at length left behind, we climbed the steep ascent leading to the flat-topped hill on which Helpmakaar is situated. The hill is steep enough to have given a name to the village, Helpmakaar being the Dutch words "*help-ma-kaar*,"— "help my cart up," as it runs in English. Once at the top, the road is carried along the summit of the hill, and is perfectly level for some twenty-five miles, thus giving an idea of the size of the hills in South Africa.

The towns and villages in that country are for the most part mere names in capitals on the map. Umsinga, just passed, consists of a small store the size of an Irish cabin, and a missionary's house distant quite two miles. Helpmakaar exists only since the present war, one small farm having previously marked the spot laid down for the village on the map. During the early part of the war it became a place of great importance; but typhoid fever gradually gaining ground among the troops there, it had to be abandoned. When we marched through, it was merely used as a hospital for those cases too ill to bear removal, and as a depot for Rorke's Drift. There were also in camp the remnants of the 1st battalion 24th Regiment —fine, stalwart men, bearded and bronzed by the sun, till they looked in their blue guernseys more like sailors than soldiers.

Close to was the *laager*, strongly made of earth—its excessive strength being excusable when we remember its nearness to Rorke's Drift, and the terrible circumstances under which it was constructed.

Helpmakaar is only twelve miles by road from Rorke's Drift; as the crow flies, it is barely half that distance.

A short ride across the mountain will take you to a cliff looking over that now historical place. The mountain-top is a series of gently rolling swells, which, like waves, follow one another interminably. The hollows, imperceptible from a distance, deepen gradually till they become valleys, then ravines with scarped sides, many miles in length, until they end in the central valley of the Buffalo.

Nestling among the fallen boulders at the foot of these crags are the beehive-shaped *kraals* of a Kafir village, cunningly hidden, and apparently deserted. But the women are inside with the children: having spied a stranger in the distance, they have bolted within the huts, drawing the wicker door across the entrance, and lying as silent as rabbits in their holes till the intruder has left. The mountain is alive with life. Snakes are by no means rare; grey lizards rustle towards their holes, looking quite too large for the work of so small a creature; larks and other small birds are springing around; the graceful Kafir crane stalks grandly away; a covey of partridges get up from the long grass and whir loudly over the ground; a secretary bird is busy searching for vermin, frogs, snakes, and suchlike, for which good service he is protected, with the vultures overhead, by the Government. One of the bustard tribe, called locally a "*paauw*," is common on these mountain-tops, and is a fine game-bird, well worth powder and shot. A larger species, not so common, attains an enormous size, often weighing over fifty pounds. Like other game here, they are easily approached on horseback, the sportsman circling round and round the bird, being careful not to look at it, and gradually lessening the diameter of the circle till he is within shot. This is called "ringing," and is generally successful, even with the most wary game. An officer at Helpmakaar saw a *paauw* struck down by an eagle, and riding up, was in time to rescue the scarcely dead bird, and take it back to mess.

Innumerable ant-hills stud the grass. How so many millions of the creatures can exist is a wonder. Our men put the nest to a practical use by cutting off the top, and hollowing it out OB one side, when it made an excellent fireplace, the substance of the nest itself burning slowly, and continuing to smoulder for a long time after the fuel was exhausted. So on arrival at a fresh camping-ground there was a general rush after ant-hills, and many amusing scenes were enacted by the lucky ones who secured a good one, and insured its not being "jumped" by sitting on the top in-triumph.

"Jumping" is the polite term for stealing in South Africa, and is tolerably universal. Nothing, from your horse to a mealie-stalk taken from a Kafir field, is safe, and the institution is not creditable to the colony.

A short time previously a pony had been stolen from the Commander-in-chief's camp, which happened to be his own property. Officers were despatched far and near to search every camp and bring back the missing pony. It was a case of undoubted sacrilege, and punishments the most stringent were prophesied as the lot of the delinquent. Suspicion fell on the men of one particular camp, and to it the chief transport-officer went himself. Every one was asked if he knew anything of the pony; but all denied. The officer in search avowed that it was in that camp; his information was undoubted, and he could not leave until it was given up. So he commenced to unload his waggon and pitch his tent. It seemed all but hopeless, when one of his men, poking about in the bush, stumbled upon the long-lost pony, comfortably tethered out of sight behind the tent of one of those who had been most persistent in his denials. The pony was recovered, the transport-officer took down his tent and returned with the missing animal, and nothing more was said of the matter. It was a case of "jumping," that was all.

Five miles' ride across the mountain from Helpmakaar brings one to a perpendicular cliff looking down on the Buffalo, just over Rorke's Drift. The post is hidden by the ground, but the signal mountain above it, from which the Zulus fired upon the garrison, is visible, and near it the column of smoke from the post.

Beyond the deep valley at the bottom of which runs the Buffalo, is Zululand, dry and forbidding; plains running up into hill-ranges; these again surmounted by flat-topped mountains. There is no sign of life, no moving thing, no cattle, no smoke to show the villages. Near the river are a few trees; opposite, a slope, covered with grass, leading to what is now known as "Fugitives' Drift." At the bottom of this Melville and Coghill fell, and there lie buried under a stone monument cut and put up to their memories by their comrades. Once, the hillside on which we stand was a throng of fugitives running for bare life, the cruel foe following. Now, there is no living being within sight; cattle are lazily feeding on the neighbouring hills; above all shines the glorious sun. In the uninviting country across the valley, some few miles away, rises a small hill, standing alone, and just joined to the mountain-range on the left by a low neck. A cloud is over it just now, and it stands out from the rest black and ominous. The glasses showed little dots scattered over the low land which led to it; otherwise there was nothing but dark rock and dry plain. And this was Isandlwana! Some way to the left, on the hills, was the spot where the Zulu army formed up, in sight of the camp, previous to the attack. The little dots were the deserted waggons—as yet, when we looked at them, unclaimed. Ten miles or more to the right lay a range of high mountains, amongst which Lord Chelmsford's force was during the fatal day.

In our direction, by the side of a little rounded hill, had been the line of flight. The thought of the bodies of our countrymen, and of their camp, still lying as they lay that afternoon, though nearly three months were gone, was no pleasant reflection. General Funk was still a power in the colony.

Tales of the fight were everywhere to be heard.

"How lucky we are!" said an officer when the Zulus first appeared; "we shall do the whole thing ourselves, and the others, when they come back and find it over, will be awfully sold!"

Another, a survivor, said: "I was just coming back to camp

when I saw the hill black with Kafirs. The cannon began firing, but the Zulus kept pouring down on our front and on our flank. The Zulus-in front of the cannon, when they saw the gunners stand clear, either fell down or divided in the middle so as to leave a lane, and when the shot had passed, shouted out, '*Umoya*.' There was no hurry or confusion with them, but all was done as if they had been drilled to it. At last they made a simultaneous charge against us when about two hundred yards off. I had to run away, having no doubt the Zulus would catch me. I saw them killing the soldiers all round me. I was fortunate to have a horse given me, and managed to get on him and ride away. I saw a soldier running past a bush, when a Zulu sprang out and threw a broad-bladed assegai at him, which struck him between the shoulders. The soldier fell on his face, and the Zulu ran up to him, and calling out '*Usutu*,' stabbed him to the heart with the same assegai. When I came to the precipice it was twelve feet high, but I shut my eyes and jumped my horse over it. When I got to the river there were plenty of Zulus before me, but I put spurs to the horse and got into the stream. Four or five white men got hold of my horse's tail to swim across, so that he could not move, when the Zulus ran up and assegaied some, while the rest let go and were carried away by the stream, only to be killed further down. On the bank I saw one of our Kafirs fight a Zulu. After some guarding on both sides, the Zulu stabbed our Kafir in the shoulder; thereupon the Kafir jumped up into the air and struck his assegai to the Zulu's heart, after which both of them rolled into the river. Every time the Zulus stabbed a white man they cried out 'Usutu,'—that is their war-cry. The natives heard them calling out, 'Leave the Kafirs, as the white men made them fight!' It was about seven miles we ran to the Buffalo, and the Zulus chased us for three miles across that river."

Such was the substance of most men's stories of that sad day, and it was a relief to turn away from the sight of a place bringing such recollections to our minds, and to set our faces towards the bright plateau lying between ourselves and the troops, with hearts buoyed up with such sanguine hopes of retribution and success.

West of Helpmakaar, the mountain descends to a vast sandy plain, dotted with darker patches of cultivation. The land is seamed with water-courses, with steep sides and soft sandy bottoms, over which, after rain, the water rushes in a torrent. These are called, locally, "spruits," and form a serious obstacle to travelling. Where the term "Sand" is prefixed, the stream is of sufficient importance to be named as such on the map—many dozen such "Sand Spruits " appearing are a sign of the paucity of landmarks or inhabited places in the colony.

Across this valley the Drakensberg range raises its crests to some 10,000 feet, often in the winter season covered with snow. In this range rise the Mooi and Tugela—rivers which cross the whole of Natal, until they unite and form the boundary of Lower Zululand. Beyond the mountains lies the Orange Free State, the last possession left to the Dutch in South Africa.

Strangely peaked hills, with scarped tops, pop up here and there in the landscape. Some are quite pointed, others again flat, as if their points had been sliced off level with those of their larger neighbours, so much the peculiar feature of this peculiar country.

These isolated hills are called "Kops," often adding thereto the name of some individual; so there is "Krantz Kop," "Pagadis Kop," "Mak-atees Kop," and many others, useful as points to steer by when crossing the grass flats which surround them.

Helpmakaar, and further north, is the land of horses and sheep, flocks of which are feeding everywhere; the farms here and there, each with a circular stone *kraal* for the stock to sleep in. Wool henceforth, and away into the Transvaal, is the staple of the land, and each sheep should give a fleece in weight about four pounds.

The horses, or rather ponies, are hardy, rough beasts, moving cleverly across the grass, which is generally a network of holes. Sheep and horses were in abundance on the hill-tops when we passed, but white men there were none. The farms were shut up and deserted by their owners, and Kafirs left alone in charge of the stock. Isandlwana was less than twenty miles away, and the Zulus are a race fleet of foot, and I might be amongst them within an hour. So the farmers were away, and we marched through an uninhabited country. It was along this road, over a bleak mountain-top, that Lord Chelmsford rode in hot haste after Isandlwana, anxious to reach the still unconscious colony and put it in a state of defence against the hourly-expected Zulus; and a sad ride it must have been, with that battle-field vivid before his eyes. Always a man with a kind heart, beloved by his soldiers, and loving them in return, the loss of so many known to him by sight, and often by name, was enough to break the most iron spirit, and make the owner wish to be away. Yet the General nobly performed his duty, sacrificing himself to the necessities of the situation, and his good name still lives in the colony.

The road was used equally by others riding hard, in obedience to the orders of another General, only too eager to obey him to the letter. In haste to convey intelligence to the rear, they galloped away, forgetful of everything except the present, and succeeding admirably in carrying out their orders. In the latter part of the war, "carrying intelligence to the rear" went out of fashion, and was looked upon as a service to be avoided.

Dundee lies at the end of the mountain, in a valley, and is another of the towns existing only on the map. A farmhouse, snugly placed on the slope of a hill; two stores, as many miles apart; and a tiny brick house, which is a church, —make up the entire place. It is, however, the centre of a flourishing district, and having been chosen as the rendezvous of the central column, was crowded during the war. Troops of all arms of the service were there in camp by hundreds, soldiers were everywhere, volunteers abounded, every pocket had money in it, and the stores did a roaring trade. It also possesses some seams of most excellent coal, which was a great luxury after the want of fuel we had experienced through the scarcity of wood in the colony.

It is remarkable how various countries get accustomed to certain things by particular makers, supplied to them by the shops. Habit has given each its own tastes, its likes and dislikes, its favourite brands and manufacturers. You may go into every shop in a colony and find each one supplied with precisely the same things as the last. In India, before the Mutiny, the brandy must be Exshaw's; Coward supplied the tinned provisions; Allsopp the bottled beer; while no shop or pedlar was complete without Macassar oil, tapes, and seidlitz-powders. In Mauritius, Martel supplies the brandy, Younger the beer, Moir the tinned meats; while the shops all sell cigars at ten for sixpence, highly-coloured liqueurs, and Gruyere cheese.

Now, in Natal, Hennesy supplies brandy, Bass the beer, Morton the tinned things of every conceivable kind; while Hollands gin, or "square-face," in red boxes and square bottles, is in every house and hovel. The stores are provided invariably with jams, olive-oil, small basins, gaudy chintz, brown corduroy, beads, saddles Warranted to give sore backs, bamboos for whip-handles, baskets made by the Kafirs to carry native beer, vial-bottles of patent medicines with such strange names as "Cajeput Olie" and "Borst Droppels." Besides these are a wonderful assortment of sweets—"snowdrops," "ripe pears," "Ching Changs," "Argyle stars," "locomotive drops," and so on for twenty labels. Of these the Boers are immensely fond; and you see a big yellow-bearded fellow in a slouch-hat and velvet "cords" buying half a pound of the sticky things, just as a child in England does her ha'porth of acid-drops.

Liquor is of course an indispensable adjunct, and is sold across the counter everywhere at a shilling a glass. "Square-face" is the invariable stuff, and you take as much as you like for a glass, though it is thought bad taste to fill up above the "pretty." Guzzling is thus encouraged to a dreadful extent. Every store is full of half-sodden men, who lounge about it the whole day, and persist in entering into conversation on the smallest pretext. "Square-face" is the bane of the colony, never absent; and till a change comes over the fondness of the colonists —almost to a man in the rural districts given to it—so long will the colony retain its present half-starved condition.

Postal arrangements had been sadly deranged by the war, and the additional mass of letters and in a little place like Dundee were little short of chaos. The post-office, adapted to the half-a-dozen letters a-week passing through in peace-time, found itself suddenly filled with the correspondence of some half-dozen regiments. The mail might go out to-morrow if a Kafir could be found to carry it; and there was another expected to-day; it ought to have been in yesterday,—and so on, as a young man, got up in riding-boots and spurs, informs you, condescending to look in at the office from the counter next door, where he is selling much "square-face" to the usual crowd of idlers-about. Stamps are an impossibility. For a few shillings I bought up the whole stock, and a more filthy and crumpled lot of bits of paper I never handled. Subsequently, during the advance, military post-offices were formed, and we got our letters with some show of regularity—all going free in the colony, owing to the thoughtful generosity of the Government.

Chapter Eight
Life in Camp

The three infantry regiments told off to the Second Division arrived about the same time, with two batteries of artillery, and the usual allowance of Engineers and Commissariat. Ten days must then pass at the least before the 17th Lancers and 1st Dragoon Guards could arrive; and after that, it was a matter of doubt if the Division would start for a further ten days or more. So all our hurry in leaving Durban and marching up country was thrown away, and we were proportionately discouraged.

Then came a whisper—growing louder every time it was repeated, until it became a certainty amongst us—that forts were to be constructed at ten-mile intervals on the road to Ulundi, each one to be garrisoned by men of one of the regiments of our Division; and nothing else was talked about but the chances of each of them being the unlucky one. Thus a second scare began, and took away still more enthusiasm with it.

About,this time arrived General Newdigate, who was to lead the Division to Ulundi. His round face, and short light hair and whiskers, gave him a smart appearance, which took with all of us at once. He was, as a man said, "ready for anything." He was a little man, pleasant to talk to, rather fond of laying down the law, and always dressed in the neatest of uniforms. His buff- leather straps over both shoulders and round his waist were spotless, and his gold-banded cap shone throughout the campaign with untarnished lustre. We liked him, men and officers, and were only sorry that Lord Chelmsford's presence with the Division allowed him no opportunity of proving his soldier-like abilities.

The General, like many others, had his own idea of the Zulus, and at an inspection he made of the infantry at Dundee, put them through the usual Aldershot attack-drill modified by himself, winding up by telling the men, who straggled up breathless and upset by the rough ground, ant-hills, ditches, and mud-holes after the final "charge," that "this was the only way to advance against an overwhelming fire"—a totally new and somewhat disconcerting aspect of the enemy's tactics, against which we had been taught to stand in "close order," and give them the bayonet freely, as their fire was all rubbish. They were infamous shots, their firearms were mostly worthless, and they invariably put up the "sight" to its highest point, under the idea that the piece gained strength in shooting by the practice,—all of which we found was quite true in the future.

While waiting for the order to advance, a remarkable instance of the discovery of crime by circumstantial evidence occurred. The men of one of the regiments had been paid, each man receiving five shillings, the money being distributed in sovereigns, one to each group of four men, owing to the scarcity of silver. The recipient of one of the sovereigns happened to drop it in his tent, and though assisted by two comrades who were there at the time, never found it again. A complaint was lodged with the captain by the man who had lost his money, and it was remembered that a somewhat similar case took place on board the ship coming out, a man having dropped half-a-sovereign, which he was unable to find, being assisted by one of the two men who had so willingly given their services on the present occasion. Fortunately there were no shops at which the men could buy—there was only a regimental canteen in camp; and orders were given to the sergeant in charge of it to watch, and take a note of any money spent by the two men who had assisted in the search after the missing coin. That evening the man suspected of the theft on board swaggered in and changed a sovereign, spending fully half of it in drink. It was then easy to prove that he had not" been honestly in possession of such a coin at the time, and the theft was clearly brought home to him, and with it the usual, indeed the only punishment, flogging.

Notwithstanding all that has been said lately about this punishment, it must always remain in force with an army constituted now, as ours is, of the lowest class. In the field especially it must hold its own, no other deterrent being

60

available. The nonsense that is talked of its debasing effects on the character of the men, is in practice mere sentiment. The cases of good men being flogged are so rare as to be almost unknown. To a bad character the penalty is compensated by the knowledge that if he bears it manfully he will become a considerable hero in the eyes of his comrades—a kind of reward not to be got out of any kind of imprisonment. The man who can take punishment in such a manner as to elicit admiration, will certainly make a better soldier in the field than one whose feelings are so tender as to break down at the appearance of pain. Men of late have been educated too much for the barrack-room, forgetful that the ultimate use of the soldier is on the field, hard and rough, death-strewn, with scenes of pain around so frequent as to be unnoticed. It can be further asserted as true that there is no spectacle which an officer dislikes more than a flogging, and yet there is hardly an officer in the army who would vote for its abolition.

Camp-life, into which we appeared to have dropped all at once, was dull work after the march, and many were the expedients to pass the time. Cooking became a great resource— the necessities of the situation required it; and all sorts of dishes were tried, and shown about in triumph. The man whose dinner was a little better than usual, talked about it, and got certain credit for his cleverness. An oven sunk in the ground, and closed in with the lid of a tin box, bore off the Cordon of honour. Stews were in great request, as they contained food and drink in one—their popularity being much increased by the discovery that meat will not assume the consistency of leather if simmered gently, instead of being boiled as fast as the fire will let it.

The only occupied farm near gave us excellent milk for sixpence a bottle, and a few disreputable-looking Kafirs ventured in of a morning with more, too dirty for use, and some fowls, which were eagerly bought up. One officer was lucky enough to buy seven, forgetting the difficulty of keeping live-stock in an open camp where "jumping" was the rule and honesty the exception, but eventually solving the question by putting the birds into a bag, and hanging it at night to his tent-pole. These were indeed days of luxury compared with the months that followed.

The scraps of conversation heard in passing through the tents were often curious. Says Brown to his friend Jones, who has dropped in for an evening chat—

"Have a cup of cold tea, old boy?" and to him answers Jones, in a sad and tragic voice—

"Brown, if you'd said that to me at Aldershot, I'd have knocked you down; but now I don't mind if I do."

Robinson, a portly captain, pokes his head into Smith's tent, and in tones not to be taken lightly, demands the return of a candle lent some days before—retiring happy and consoled, candle in hand.

"Where's the salt, Murphy?" cries a third, with angry voice.

"You've ate it up, sor!" exclaims the man.

"Well, give my compliments to Major Johnston, and ask him to lend me a pinch."

These and similar scraps represented the usual conversation in camp.

But sooner than was expected a forward movement was made, and it was decided to occupy Conference Hill, some thirty miles towards the front, as the new base of operations.

The regiment chosen was the 94th, and it started,-not without envy from those left behind, payed out of camp by the bagpipes of the 21st, almost a month since it landed at Durban. It was a pretty picture, and one fraught with hope to all of us, as the long, sinuous line, more than a mile in length, wound across the neck of land separating two hills on our front, which had till now blocked out the wished-for Zululand. The old farmer and his wife from whom we had bought the milk, came out of their tree-shaded cottage, the last we were to see for many months, and waved the regiment farewell; the regiments gave a parting cheer, and every man in the departing line put his best foot foremost, now he felt he was really going to the front.

A guide was required, for the road was one seldom used,

leading only to the half-dozen Dutch farms which lie in the debatable ground between the Buffalo and the Blood rivers. Landsman's Drift, then a mere spot on the prevailing grass-land, but destined soon to be one of the army's principal bases, lies on the former river, there a slow-running stream of clear water between high and difficult banks—a boundary-line which brought the regiment to a halt for the night.

Across the river could be seen one or more farmhouses, now deserted, and a native *kraal* or so burnt, their places being known by fields of Indian corn waving in the wind, and the stone cattle *kraals* with which each one is provided. A troop of ownerless ponies send out the mounted men, and after a hard ride one is caught; while on the river a flock of tame geese, wild now, made capital shooting for those lucky enough to have guns. Everywhere is a rolling plain of grass, except in front, where rises abruptly, barely a mile away, the great mass called by the Dutch Doornberg, or Thorn Hill. Hardly had the troops arrived when they were met by a veritable old man of the mountain, or Rip Van Winkle. He was mounted on a sorry little pony, and wore a long white beard. His face was piebald with red and purple patches, and his clothes were worn and disreputable. The apparition announced himself as a farmer of the neighbourhood with important information, and asked for "square-face." This being supplied, he let out his information. A Zulu "*Impi*" was constantly quartered within a few miles of our right flank; a second *Impi* had heard of our intended advance to the Blood river, and lay across our way. If we persevered in our present intentions, a fight must follow, and in those days the results of any such rashness were considered to belong, as a matter of course, to the enemy. The intelligence was sufficiently authentic to warrant a messenger being despatched hot haste to Dundee, asking what was to be done under such critical circumstances—a message replied to by an order which sent the troops on their way truly, but by a circuitous road round Doornberg, thereby losing a day's march, and presenting a flank instead of a front to the expected attack. In the days to come we were not so apt at believing the stories of semi-drunken farmers, and estimated at its proper value the Zulu *Impi*, for long the bogy of the British. The Impi itself is formidable enough, and requires special knowledge to stand against; but it is but a mass of human beings like ourselves, and is incapable of turning up at all times, and in every place, like a Jack-in-the-box.

The method used by the Zulus to collect an *Impi* was to send round word to the villages, ordering the men to assemble at the king's *kraal* on a certain day, usually about new moon; a grand ceremony of doctoring and savage rites then took place, and the Impi was despatched to some given spot. Once in motion it moved with enormous speed, and was at the given place to a moment, and in magnificent fighting order. But fight or not, that accomplished, the task set it was done, and the host melted away—returning each one to his own village, some few to the king with an account of their doings; and, wish it however he might, the king could not induce the Impi to collect again until a given time. Like all natives of Africa, they wanted change, wished for the enjoyments of their homes, were anxious to tell their deeds of daring there, and receive the praises of their women; while, above all, the arrangements for feeding them when on the war-path were not calculated for more than three days.

Yet hardly a day passed that General Funk did not report the presence of an *Impi* as immment.

A whole day was taken up in crossing the Buffalo—none too much for the number of waggons the column had to convoy. The drift was formed by the banks on either side being cut away into steep slopes, at a spot where the river-bed was smooth and hard. The soldiers were marched down to the stream by companies, and taking off boots, socks, and trousers, waded across, as some said, just like ready-made Highlanders. The waggons, each with a double team of oxen, jolted at a run down the near incline, and entered the water with a splash, and, amid a chorus of cracking whips, groans, and cries, such as none but Kafirs can give out, crawled up the far one. Conductors on ponies galloped backwards and forwards; the transport officer shouted himself hoarse; and every one was busy from early morning till dusk, when the unwieldy vehicles were all across and safely in *laager* on the other side.

Amusing incidents were not wanting. An unfortunate non-combatant, here manifestly against his will, and sorely mistrusting the powers of his pony, supplied by Government, to face the stream, made several heroic attempts down the bank, but retreated each time before his steed wetted his feet; till, wearied out at last by the laughter he provoked, he was forced to accept another person's hand, and was so led across the water in mild triumph.

The march lay through the valley of the Buffalo, a much -winding river in a broad expanse of grass. Close on the right hand rose Doornberg, green to the summit, which was irregular and flat; some miles on the left a range of hills across the river. The grass often rose to our shoulders, and the soldiers pushing through it looked thoroughly picturesque; path there was none, — the line just followed an old waggon-track, or the marks made by our Engineers, who preceded us earlier in the morning.

Far out on this sea of grass we had been watching a speck moving constantly, which might be a horse-, an ox, or some wild animal. The glasses made it out to be like an ox; to imaginations fired with accounts of South African sport, it was a wild buffalo. So a sportsman was soon in the saddle, and rode off with a rifle to solve the question. His progress was eagerly watched: the leaving the pony in a hollow, which instantly galloped home—the stalk, and the final shot, when the great beast fell over heavily,—were all intensely interesting. Our anticipations of sport were, however, rudely shattered when the sportsman returned with the news that he had only shot a tame ox, wandering about ownerless on the veldt. Like other things, we got to know even what this meant after a time,—learning that cattle in this country are very liable to a disease called "lung sickness," when they become useless, and are allowed to wander where they like over the almost boundless plains till they fall and die.

Gazing over this expanse of grass-land, entirely level to the eye, we were told that Zululand was but a continuation of the same; and the thought at once occurred to most, "What a splendid cavalry country, and how ours will score when they ride over it!" Yet experience soon taught us it was rather the reverse. Flat to the eye, on travelling over it you will find it a succession of huge rolling swells, in which the grass-land rises and falls almost interminably. The valleys between frequently hold at their lowest level a marshy stream, almost invisible even when quite near you—its sides boggy and sloppy, capable of taking in a horse bodily, and yet giving no indication of their danger by a difference of vegetation. Deserted cattle-*kraals*, now mere heaps of stones, are very common; and being hidden up by a growth of luxuriant grass, are often unnoticed until the horse is amongst them. Holes made by lizards or ant-bears are everywhere—true pitfalls for the unwary; while the ants' nests themselves, though visible enough, are so numerous as to make the ride of a single horseman a regular zigzag; to keep in formation among them is nearly impossible.

But the real and unavoidable obstacle to riding is the "donga." The term is now well known in England; yet its features, as seen in the true type of donga met with in Zululand, are hardly yet understood. In Natal, all small valleys, water-courses, and depressions of the ground are called generally dongas. It is only in the northern part that the true donga is to be found— exception being made to the coast country. But it is Zululand that they flourish and abound in.

The *donga* proper is not a ravine, a gully, or a crevasse; it is actually a distinct thing—a *donga*. Dongas appear in the most unlikely places, and are often modest, hiding themselves in grass or amongst stones, and only to be stumbled upon by accident.

To picture a donga, one must imagine a thick slice taken bodily out of the earth; the slice itself has utterly disappeared, leaving in its place a yawning gulf. This may be from a dozen to a hundred feet across; its sides are absolutely perpendicular, with buttresses here and there, always sharp as knife-edges, jagged and irregular, the opening almost as though one had laid two cross-cut saws on the ground, the teeth pointing at one another, the whole of the earth between them being removed.

The chasm thus described will be from ten to thirty feet deep, the actual bottom flat, but varied by irregular columns of earth mixed with stones, always hard and always pointed. The sides are sharp cut as with a knife, quite precipitous, and with no sign of fallen debris at the bottom. To finish the description, the donga is always a fair length, usually forming a radiation from a principal one of the series—the shorter ones a hundred yards or so in length, the longer ones frequently a mile or more.

To cross a *donga* on foot is difficult, and can only be managed by following its course till you meet a native track, which will always take you across the only place possible. To cross on horseback is impossible, unless the native paths are well marked, or the sides have become worn by the action of the weather,— not a frequent circumstance. I believe the *donga* is peculiar to South Africa. The action forming one is evidently subterranean. Water—probably from a hidden spring, or collected suddenly in the frequent thunderstorms—percolates through the earth; at a- distance from the surface the soil is dissolved away, and the mass above sinks a foot or so. This subsidence is seen at the head of most dongas, the line of subsidence being guided partly by the action of the water below, and partly by the surface cracks. Fresh percolation ensues, and the earth again sinks, till some heavy fall of rain takes place, when the whole mass, already loosened, is torn away and carried bodily down the hill.

When it is necessary to take a waggon across a donga, there are two courses open; one to go sufficiently far up the hill or valley side to head it off—the other to go low enough to where, by age and water-action, its sides have become sufficiently abraded to allow of a ramp being ? cut down one and up the opposite one.

At the northern extremity of Doornberg was a party of the 80th Regiment, snugly quartered in an earthen fort they had made for themselves, and engaged in cutting down and sending away to the front the prickly mimosa-trees which studded this end of the mountain, and ministered most gratefully to the wants of the troops in this country, so entirely destitute of trees. On the return of the Dutch proprietors of this part of

Natal at the close of the war, a new name should be chosen for their mountain, the "thorns" having almost entirely gone for firewood during the months which it lasted.

Chapter Nine
Blood and Buffalo

It was about this time that our second scare took place, and it is worth telling, as an illustration of the pitch to which officers and men had been needlessly worked up, being ready to magnify the smallest incident into an attack by the omnipresent Zulus.

About eight in the evening, when the troops were safely in their tents inside the *laager*, several shots were heard at no great distance, and the men were at once got under arms. The *laager* was strengthened, the wheels of the waggons locked, the opening secured, and squads of men, rifles in hand, told off to their places, —some on the waggons, others underneath.

Meanwhile a party of irregular horse, under Captain Bettington, which was attached to the column, was sent out in the direction of Zululand, some few miles distant, to reconnoitre. It was a bright moonlight night, and the *laager*, bristling with steel, looked impregnable, as indeed it was. Hour after hour passed without the return of the patrol, or the sign of any hostile Zulus. A staff officer venturing outside for a look round was thought rash in the extreme, and very venturesome to risk his life so wantonly. Another officer following his example was recalled to his post inside with stern decision. At last the patrol returned. It had been miles round the frontier and along the Blood river, and had not seen a living soul. Then one hitherto silent, emboldened by the evident absence of the enemy, suggested that certain boxes on the sides of our waggons, on being shut quickly, might have given out the noise of shots fired. The boxes were applied to, and the lids being slammed, gave out a distinct series of shots, fired at just the distance at which the original ones had been heard. The mystery was solved, and the men, chilled and humbugged, crept back into their blankets.

The worst part of the Blood river is its name. In itself it was, when we came up to it in May, a slow-running stream, some fifteen feet in breadth, twisting considerably more than is considered necessary by well-regulated streams, through a vast grass meadow. The banks were high and the bottom muddy, so that it forms a slight obstacle to an advance, which the Zulus, as yet, had appeared disinclined to cross.

The column, marching from Landman's Drift, found the river totally deserted, its tents the first sign of life at a place shortly to bristle with armed men, forts, stores, and waggons, known as Conference Hill. Our camp and the inevitable *laager* were made on the slope of a long spur of grass-land, trending down from a curious terraced hill, which is that of Conference, to the river. At the end of this spur were the white marquees and piles of stores, hourly increasing, belonging to the Commissariat, and forming the nucleus of three months' supply for the army. On either side of these a company of Engineers were busy building two square forts to protect the supplies.

Across the river, almost invisible between its steep banks, were the blackened remains of a *kraal*, with the lines of intrenchment made by Wood's column in the January previous. Above these rose Bemba's Kop, a rounded hill with scarped and rocky sides, sticking straight out of the plain. On the top were posted two scouts, sent from the Native Contingent, their black bodies dark and distinct against the sky; and beyond all, a rolling sea of yellow grass, leading up to a range of mountains, from whose recesses the smoke of Zulu fires was constantly ascending: and this was Zululand, and our onward way across it.

To the left the fires of Wood's camp at Kambula flung their smoke over a second range, Zlobane among them in the far east. In rear from the hill-top could be seen the tents at Balder's Spruit, where detachments of the 80th and 13th Regiments kept his communications open with Utrecht. Close behind the camp was a small farmhouse belonging to one of the Piet Uys' family, but now deserted. It was but a ruin, after all: the roof was gone, every scrap of furniture had disappeared, and the grove of blue gums which surrounded it were rapidly falling under the axes of the soldiers. One solitary mimosa weathered the storm for some time on the hillside opposite, until one morning it fell a victim to the universal want of fuel, and made the acquaintance of the company's cook.

The Dutch are said to have named the river after a great victory over the Zulus, when they defeated their army with great loss, the honest "*vrows*" doing good service by chopping off the hands of the savages as they tried to climb into the *laager*. The bodies were afterwards thrown into the river, which ran red for some days in consequence. Some time in July the Boers rally at the hill above our camp, and celebrate the anniversary of the victory. The tale rests entirely on tradition, which never loses in the telling.

Between the Buffalo and Blood rivers the strip of land has more than once been a disputed possession, and was naturally imported into the history of the late war.

So far back as 1861, two of Cetewayo's brothers, flying from his anger, took refuge at Utrecht, a town inside the Transvaal borders. The Dutch, at his request, gave the unfortunate men up, receiving as their reward a good slice of Zululand proper, which lies east of the Blood river, and across which our camp looked. After some years it suited Cetewayo to deny this agreement—a lesson to those who are partial to treating savages as men and brothers; and he turned to Natal, strongly urging on the Government the manifest advantage that would accrue to it if it took possession of the land under dispute. This was in 1870. Natal, however, would not accede, but sent a Commission to inquire into the whole boundary question thus opened up. The inquiry dragged along after the halfhearted way common to such measures, till the Zulu, sharp enough to see his advantage in others' indecision, increased his claims so as to include a tract of country undeniably under the Transvaal Republic, the strip which lies between the two rivers among the rest, together with a portion belonging to an independent tribe, our late allies, the Swazies. Thus pushed into a corner, the Commission awarded to Cetewayo the Blood river as an extreme boundary westward, with the Pongola as his northern limit—ignoring entirely his claims upon territory not his own, but his neighbours. The award not being to his liking— in which he had hoped, indeed, to find the English as dishonest as himself—he commenced a series of raids and hostile demonstrations, which in the end rendered the late war necessary.

On arriving at the Buffalo, each corps had established a rigid system of outposts, by day and night—a system only abandoned when the war was at an end, and quite as fatiguing and as much disliked by all ranks. The day outposts were shortly given up; indeed they should never have been instituted, the cavalry vedettes round a camp being sufficient to give warning of approaching danger. But then in those first days General Funk was a great authority, and most of the useless and irritating orders of that time can be traced to his interference.

Night outposts are most necessary, and at the same time the most disagreeable duty which a soldier is called upon to perform. In the late war the duty was the greatest hardship of the campaign. The first night I was on outpost duty the moon was shining brilliantly, and the sky-line was sharp and distinct as by day. The bayonets were fixed, and rifles loaded. What orders were necessary were given in a low, serious tone, "To keep a sharp look-out for the enemy over the ridge : if only a few men are seen, send back word at once; if more, fire—and fire low!" The poor sentry's answer to my "Do you understand me?" was low and serious too, as he turned away to pace his lonely and dangerous post.

Some, on giving up their orders to the patrol, mixed them queerly: one, I remember, said he had to look out for any "crowds or bunches of men a-crawling and a-creeping forenent me post;" while another, surprised unawares, gave the reason of his inattention that "he was watching a horse coming out of a tree."

On the night I was on outpost duty, about one in the morning, a man came in breathless from the front to say that there were some half-dozen men creeping towards the line of sentries. So-off we went with a patrol, stealing up cautiously towards the crouching forms, black and distinct, against the sky, till we got to near quarters, when they melted away like phantoms, and were no more seen by us, passing on to Landman's Drift, and stealing eighteen head of cattle from the too confident troops there. Hardly had we taken the patrol back when the moon went in behind the thick fog-wreaths which came rolling up the valley, and in a few seconds every landmark was swathed in white mist, and utterly hidden. To leave one's lair by the reserve was to wander helplessly over the dim-lighted plain, or to get entangled in the windings of the river, its water meeting you silently out of the reeds and dripping bulrushes, with a cold glare at each fresh turning. The long grass was soppy with water; boots and clothing were quickly soaked. One stumbled against ant-hills, or fell bodily into holes or bogs, till hope itself fled, and a dead halt ensued, the feeling creeping over one's numbed body of being totally, helplessly lost. Then, when all was blank despair, the distant cry of a sentry in the *laager*, half a mile away, came across the fog, and we knew where we were, and started once more, stumbling and tumbling, till brought up by the rough challenge of our sentry, his bayonet-point within an inch or two of our limp bodies. After that came long hours, wet and cold, weary and sleepy, till the relief arrived at eight o'clock, and we shivering ones, with boots full of water, got away to the tents like the proverbial drowned rats. Yet this was only a nightly specimen of a Zulu fog for months to come.

That there were parties of the enemy sneaking about after plunder during the nights, was not only most probable, considering the habits of the people, but was further shown up by the events of the very next night, when the midnight wanderers caused scare number three in the *laager*, to which came in breathless, as usual, a messenger from the guard, to say that a party was to be seen crawling up towards it. The bugles rang out the "alert," the men tumbled anywhere in their hurry, bayonets flashed in the moonlight, the loose ammunition rattled in the pouches ready for action, the breeches of the rifles clicked ominously as they were loaded, and in came the outposts at the double, a fat sergeant well in rear, panting, and dropping with perspiration and terror. Then followed some irregular shots from our own guards outside, who shortly after came inside also; and the certainty of some real work at last brought out a flush of excitement on many faces. Then came a rush of our own natives pouring into the *laager*, assegais and shields in hand, and abject funk on their faces, their bodies muffled up in a blanket, all eager to dive under the nearest waggon as the safest place, from which refuge they were as quickly pushed out again by the kneeling ranks there already. In came, too, half-a-dozen of our mounted volunteers, stuck round with cartridges, and maudlin with drink. A shot inside the now crowded *laager*. followed, then a short struggle; it might have been Zulus for all any one knew, but was only the interpreter, strangely attired in a semi-military dress, clutching a rifle from which the smoke was still issuing, and protesting loudly. In his excitement, or worse, he had loaded and fired straight away into the thick of us, the bullet being dug out next morning under the feet of the guard itself. But a sharp volley at that moment made us forget him and his freak; for an instant the night was lit up with the flash, and men said to each other that it had come at last. One I saw cleverly lay his helmet down beside him, and, taking out his ammunition, open the packets, and empty his whole seventy rounds into it, ready for action.

But we waited for another long and in vain; the echoes died out unanswered, not a sign of living thing was there outside our face of the *laager*, and after a time the whole coast was reported clear; the party, whatever it was, had gone away, and we went back to our beds once more. Next morning two oxen, standing alone outside the *laager*, refused to turn out with the rest to graze; their legs, wounded in the late scare, declined to carry them. Poor beasts! they alone had fallen victims to our first volley in Zululand.

Camp "shaves" relieved the monotony of our life a little; but delay, seemingly without end, worked upon the men, and made them and officers dull and dispirited. So any talk of a move was eagerly caught at. Wood's officers, often through the camp, brought the newest, and it did much to make men forget the stupidity of so many scares. It was, that their column was to march some few miles parallel to our own in a general advance in about ten days' time on Ulundi. The march was to be pushed on with all despatch; and when the columns came near the *kraal*, the Lancers were to ride ahead, burn it, and return, after which the whole would retire into Natal. Not a soldier was to be in Zululand after 20th June. Should the attack be unsuccessful, all were to go into winter quarters at Maritzburg, and wait till next year, or at least until November.

Alas, our ten days expanded into a month I and on the given day in June by which we were all to be out of the country, we were just contemplating the advance towards Ulundi, still some fifty miles away. Just then, too, Lord Chelmsford paid the camp a visit, accompanied by the Prince Imperial and General Wood, and to tell the truth, met with small enthusiasm. Yet there was no distrust entertained as to his ability to beat the Zulus in the best way possible with such a slippery foe; men met him coldly because they were sick of the delay for which he got the credit, when it would have been more just had they blamed those about him for want of energy, and loitering by the way. The war in the old colony was a mere picnic, and gave a general a capital opportunity of obliging his friends and acquaintances; but sterner stuff was needed to stand against so formidable an enemy as the Zulus proved themselves. So we set out on the campaign which ended at Isandlwana as if it were but a continuation of our easy picnic-times, and when disaster overtook us, went into an opposite extreme, and doubted if success could ever be ours again.

Lord Chelmsford as often as not wore "*mufti*" —uniform was not easy to replace at the front —a light grey suit, with grey-canvas tops to his riding-boots, always kept beautifully clean; a Norfolk jacket, and a revolver slung over the shoulder, with sometimes, though rarely, a sword below. From under a rather low white helmet his anxious face peered out; a nose long and thin, and, if anything, hooked; the principal feature black bushy eyebrows, from under which his dark eyes seemed to move restlessly, ever on the watch for something sudden coming. A pleasant manner; sharp, rather jerky sentences; and a general air of watchfulness pervading all his actions. He walked quickly, turning his head from side to side, and stopping frequently to remark on some arrangement which required alteration. He gave one the idea of a man preoccupied, under a spell, and glad to get rid of his thoughts by an incessant attention to details. The sad day of Isandlwana had left its traces plainly marked on his face and manner.

Later on, when the column crossed the Umvolosi just previous to Ulundi, his face was deadly pale, and he spoke but little, seeming to be absorbed in the unknown results of the next few hours. During the battle he gave his orders calmly and firmly; his mind, depressed by the unknown, rose fearlessly to meet the danger he could see; and on all sides praises of his manner during the fight were heard. After the firing ceased, and the Zulus were in full flight, he seemed like a man with a load taken off his shoulders; his manner brightened, he laughed and chatted with those near him, and rode about praising some and speaking kindly to all. It was the happiest moment since that fatal January day, and all were sorry to lose him so soon, and under circumstances none too pleasant.

The Prince gave one the idea of a small-sized young man, with a sallow face. His manner was pleasant and open, and he was perpetually asking questions the most minute, noting the answers carefully in a book after each was given him. That he was brave and bold there was no question; though rashness would have been in English eyes the better term for his wish to accompany every trifling reconnoitring party towards the front.

Behind them rode General Wood; and Buller, the leader of his cavalry, all irregulars, almost the most useful troops for the work.

The former is a tall, thin man—like Lord Chelmsford, in *mufti*. His face is long, and ends in a short pointed beard. He also looks about nervously. His features are browned by exposure to the sun, and his manner is cheerful but decided.-With his column he was far more popular than the General was with the Division, allowing men under him to settle matters of detail as they pleased, so long as the general dispositions were observed. It was the fashion to say that, were he in supreme command, he would make small work of the Zulus, and that his column alone was quite strong enough to beat them,—ideas hardly borne out by subsequent events, when his column gradually got nearer to the Division as Ulundi approached, until at the crossing of the Umvolosi the two bodies joined together for the final struggle.

Buller was likewise dressed in *mufti*, rather seedy, with a grey wideawake hat, tied round by a bit of red cloth, the badge of the volunteers. His face is thin; his manner taciturn, not given to many words except when needed, and then sharp and decisive enough. By him rode Lord William Beresford—" Bill Beresford," as he is usually called — in a most correct suit of *mufti*. He sported a scanty crop of light whiskers and beard, and was easily known amongst the rest by his Elwood helmet and grey silk puggaree, used by the staff in India.

The officer in rather worn uniform is Colonel Harrison, the Quartermaster-General. He, too, is thin, very thin, with an expression of trouble and hard work sitting on the lines of his face. He worked hard at road-finding,—no easy task across the trackless hills of Zululand, and one, at times, quite hopeless. The inevitable donga was always in the way. Out before daylight, he was seldom to be seen in camp till late in the afternoon.

A younger man, with a square figure, and bushy black whiskers and beard, was Carey, in those days busy with a compass and surveying-block setting out the positions.

Conference Hill was a place of considerable importance, forming the base of the centre column on its advance against the king's *kraal*. This was to take place on the Utrecht-Ulundi road—a route beautifully drawn on the official maps supplied to the army, marked with a double line, as one of the principal roads of the country, and further honoured with a descriptive report in the "Precis of Information." It crossed the Blood river some two miles above the camp, led almost straight for the northern side of the Inlhlazatsi Mountain, turning the eastern end of it, and thence leading straight south on Ulundi.

The army having once got so far north, and thus out of the direct line to the *kraal*, no more suitable or convenient route could be found. Strategy—perhaps almost unneeded against a foe like the Zulus—was the consideration which placed the army in this far-distant place, neglecting the far nearer and more direct roads by Middle and Rorke's Drifts. Its selection "covered the Transvaal;" and so time and energy were wasted, while the science of strategy was observed.

So Conference Hill became a formidable position. Two stone forts, with faces twenty yards long, and surrounded by a V-shaped ditch, were constructed on either side of the incessantly increasing mountains of stores, their fire arranged so as to cross every exposed face. Two large iron buildings were built, and filled with the more perishable things; coal was brought in daily under escort from a hill some miles inside the Zulu boundary, and an enormous abattis of firewood collected round the whole. Close by was a fort built by the 94th, with sides forty yards long, and surrounded by a ditch plentifully strewn with broken bottles. Inside were the tents and marquee of the "base hospital," doctors and other staff included. Altogether, many hundred waggon-loads of stores had been brought up and unloaded; while every day the dust from fresh convoys told us that yet they came.

Visitors were abundant; generals got quite common; officers on their way somewhere else rather a bore; newspaper correspondents an infliction. The most amusing among them was the little, short, fat, good-humoured "Figaro"—French altogether, martial somewhat, but very unacquainted with the habits of his horse, and so in frequent grief in consequence. Once, on his way to Wood's camp, he lost his way, and had to sleep out on the veldt, in a place which, to his imagination, swarmed with Zulus. So he chose a patch of long grass, and hid away in it in much fear and doubt as to what the night might bring forth. What was his horror, when it was half-gone, to find that his friendly shelter had disappeared, and he lay exposed to every eye! his horse, tied up to his side, had eaten the whole of the grass for supper. Poor little man! with the death of the Prince his own mission was over, and he followed the body home, much lamenting, and gesticulating freely. Utrecht, a straggling, out-of-the-way village some twenty-five miles away, was the only place within reach where a little dissipation could be got—the gaiety consisting of a mess in a turf hut, with beer to drink, and hovels in which a bed might possibly be obtained. So at the doors of these we went about knocking, and telling our sad tale to the Dutch people inside. For more than a month we had slept on the ground, and our bones ached for one good night's rest on a bed: would none of them take compassion on us? A great many said they would if they could, and we believed them. Houses were very full then at Utrecht, and prices ran high: I paid 3s. 6d. at a public- house for a pint of ale. A few said they would not, and they looked it. One good Samaritan at length said she would, and we blessed her and her blankets for the kindness. Her name was M'Donald, and she deserves to be remembered.

It was not until I got into the bed that I missed the lumps and stones, and realised how wretched was the life we led as far as small comforts were concerned. Yet the bedstead was very cranky, standing on three legs, the wall representing the fourth; and the sheets bore decided evidence of having been used before.

The previous night I had slept on a boulder, upon which my hip-bones pivoted alternately throughout the night—an event, by the way, not uncommon, as the earth of South Africa, for lying-down purposes, is as hard as any boulder. The tent, too, was not my own, but kindly lent by a brother officer, who turned out to do the stranger honour. In the morning his soldier-servant arranged my bath—only a hole in the earth—the sponge, soap, brushes and comb,—the whole topped by a teacup full of water, across which was laid an old tooth-brush of his master's, with which to complete my own toilet. My hostess entertained us during the evening glass of "square-face" by the customary doleful anticipations of the coming campaign; there could be only one end to it—we should be beaten, barely escaping with our lives before the redoubtable Zulu king. General Funk had been quartered for some time past in Utrecht.

The town lies under the shadow of great hills, scarped precipitously, and seamed with dongas. These are the feature of the surrounding country, and an ugly and troublesome one they are. Once leave the road, and you find yourself in a network of ravines some twenty feet deep, the sides, when not perpendicular, leaning forward, and furrowed in the most fantastic manner. All about is as dry as death, and the sun strikes on your head fiercely between the dirty grey walls. After a thunderstorm the beds of these dongas become raging torrents—impassable; in dry weather they are sandy and soft, the wheels of a waggon sinking hopelessly up to the axles.

The town itself is merely a collection of hovels, scattered about without order or regularity, the stores the only decent houses; the streets crossed by gutters of running dirty water, the walls and enclosures ornamented by a few blue-gum trees. The most noticeable thing is a number of erections in the form of gallows, with the noose dangling from the centre of each. These are used in the manufacture of "reims," which are strips of raw hide, used instead of rope throughout the Transvaal. Drunken men were a common object about the streets, notwithstanding the confiscation of all liquor by the military authorities—an order necessary enough, but for which Government had to pay heavily in damages when the war was over.

"Well, Fanny, and what can I do for you?" said one of the storekeepers from behind his counter, to a pleasant-looking young lady in deep black, who came in just then. The lady was one of the daughters of Piet Uys, killed just a month previously at the Zlobane, and appeared quite used to the tone of familiarity used by the shopman. Equality takes strange modes of asserting itself in the Transvaal.

Utrecht is also rich in Kafir belles, and the shops are thronged with them, their ample forms dressed in the scantiest of clothing.

They tousle up their wool with red earth, the married ones twisting it in a round thick bunch behind—not becoming. Some wear a blanket over one shoulder, and a bead girdle round their middle, so that a view from behind leaves little to the imagination—a pair of legs, stout and sturdy, quite innocent of any covering, completing their costume.

A couple of miles outside the town was the *kraal* where Oham, Cetewayo's brother, who gave himself up to Wood early in the war, was permitted to live in ease and idleness, surrounded by his numerous wives.

At a visit I paid him at that time, I found him taking his evening stroll, accompanied by three truculent-looking Zulus armed with assegais.

Oham is a fat, sensual-faced man, and wore, when I saw him, nothing but a gaudy blanket of the favourite "chessboard" pattern over one shoulder. His features were stolid and impassive, frequently holding forward one ear as we spoke to him in English—to explain that he did not understand. The conversation was thus not over-much enjoyed, till I mentioned the magic word "square-face," of which he is known to be immoderately fond, when a genial smile burst out from his hitherto stupid face, and his hand crept stealthily out of his blanket over his fat stomach, with his fingers outspread ready to grasp the promised stuff. His heart thus opened, we were asked into his private *kraal*, following him on hands and knees through the low opening, and sitting in the dark and dismal den, while some of his wives, ranged round the opposite side, gave out a native chant.

In the little book of information published officially, and served out to each officer, the Natal Zulu is described as "an intelligent and precocious boy, with the physical strength of a man." The description is concise, but hardly does the subject full credit, as the following trait will show. Utrecht grows capital cabbages, and for some nights the mess-table had been graced by one or more of these delicacies. But one day the cabbage was not there as usual, and the Kafir boy who provided the dinners was called in and asked how it was that he had been so remiss as to forget the cabbage. "Master," replied that ingenuous one, "nights too much light got now; when moon go away, me catchee plenty more cabbage!"

But all this while time went on. It was now nearly two months since we landed, and still Zululand was to come. The delay seemed interminable. The stores increased in bulk daily; surely there were more than we could carry as it was. A correspondent, as usual with more knowledge of matters than any one else, spread the scare that the horses ate up the forage as fast as it arrived, or very nearly, the arrivals being only a few loads in excess of those consumed. From stragglers we learnt that the Division was all on the spot ready for action; the cavalry and most of the infantry at Land-man's Drift, the rest wood-cutting at Doornberg. Everywhere ennui had seized upon all, men and officers, not so long ago fired with martial ardour. Listlessness crept in, and floggings increased. Amusing incidents there were. A favourite pastime with those vested in authority was to sound the alarm, and note the time which it took the men to dress, pull down their tents, and run into the *laager*. On one such occasion, as usual, a hint was given that the alarm would sound at 4 P.M., but that it was only a case of drill, not of danger. Of course the caution filtered through the officers to the men. On the first sound of the bugle every soldier stepped out of his tent fully dressed and armed, his seventy rounds at his waist, his rifle in hand; down went the tents behind them as a run was made for the *laager*, in which the irrepressible one, smiling approval, and looking at his watch, remarked, as the last warrior bolted inside, "Ah, capital work! three minutes and twenty-five seconds! No chance for the Zulus with us." And indeed there was not, providing always that they sent us notice of their intentions an hour before they attacked.

Small reconnaissances were frequent, at most of which the Prince assisted, doing a little fighting on his own account, at a risk to himself hardly equal to the occasions—a few *kraals* burnt within sight of the frontier, a native or two killed, an old woman interviewed, and a few scraggy cocks brought in, representing the general results. One of these on a larger scale, under Buller, did more service by bringing in a report of the country passed over; while a second one, under General Marshall, to Isandlwana, fairly drove the natives who infested the place away, and recovered some forty waggons.

Chapter Ten
The Death of a Prince

Fortunately for our peace of mind, already sorely tried, the letters from correspondents had not then been published in the English papers. We only read them long afterwards, when the events they commented on had passed away with our own disgust at delays, of which we could not see the end.

The '*Natal Witness*,' a colonial paper, renowned for the outspoken character of its remarks, was our only means of knowing what was going on in the neighbourhood of the war. Its columns, cleverly written, abused pretty near all alike, and so afforded what little entertainment there was. It was in advertisements, however, that the colonial press shone. Properties for sale were often headed by some appeal from the auctioneer such as, "Here's your chance!" or "Who'd have thought it? a speedy road to a large fortune almost begging!" A colonist wants to know, in print, " the individual who, after inducing one of my coolies to abscond, drove up and tried to persuade another by offering higher wages—wanted to know the address of that gentleman." Losses are frequent, and always about "one black ox, upright horns turning inwards, swelling under jaw," or something similar. One that under our actual teetotal habits did not strike us very forcibly, was headed, "Hope for the hopeless," and puffed an "anti-bacchanalian elixir, a certain cure for the craving after alcoholic stimulants." Further on, Mr and Mrs Blank give notice that the funeral of their father will take place at such and such an hour, winding up by a paragraph in which "the Blanks beg to thank all friends for their kind sympathy."

While, sadder than all, in those early stages of the war, were often-repeated appeals as the following: "Any survivors from the Isandlwana disaster are urgently requested to supply information respecting A—B—, whose name appears among the killed. Will some of his comrades please say,—1.How and where was he? 2.Whether he escaped from the carnage to the river, or was hemmed in with those who had no ammunition to use and were killed by the Zulus? 3.Who saw him last, and under what circumstances? 4.Was he recognised after death, and was he buried? 5.Was he much mutilated, and what was the manner of his death?" Thus, as always, what was in the heart as the most important question of all was put off to the last.

With literature such as this nearly our sole resource, it was no wonder the time passed heavily. All day the men were in their shirtsleeves, unloading waggons of bags of flour, biscuit, oats; and coal. Those not so engaged were digging ditches or building forts. At night was the everlasting picket, wet, cold, and perhaps dangerous. At tattoo all had to rush into *laager*, were it wet or fine, standing with fixed bayonets in silent array till the inspecting officer had gone round. That over, lights out, and a hard night's rest on the ground, broken at an hour before daybreak by the bugles, when a fresh array in the *laager* ensued. A dreary interval, cold, wet, sleepy, and dirty, till we managed a swill in a bucket in the welcome warmth of the rising sun, and breakfast off the cold lumps of stew left over from last night's dinner. After that, more waggons to off-load, and more ditches to dig. No wonder we wanted to get on, even against such terrible fellows as the Zulus. Our awakening came at last, changing everything that had been arranged, and showing us that all our work of the past month was so much labour wasted.

Conference Hill was no longer to be the base of operations: the advance was by another road; and all the piles of stores collected there, with so much trouble and expense, were to be moved to Koppie Allein, twelve miles lower down the river. From this place the column was to cross into Zululand, and to move, by another road to the one previously selected, on Ulundi. Miles away down the river we had seen an isolated peak, sticking up just over the grass-line to the south, which was our horizon; and the reconnoitring parties had told us this was Koppie Allein—the "Lone Koppie; "but up till now there had

84

been no road thither, or any, save the troopers of Bettington's Horse, that had penetrated as far. Landman's Drift, lying closer, had supplied the new base with soldiers and stores; so that, on the last day of May, when the garrison of Conference Hill marched in, across the almost trackless *veldt*, it found it alive with military life,—a pleasant change indeed, after the weeks of inaction, and, of late, rainy weather, which blew our tents down, and sent us, cold and wet, to shelter under still damper bed-clothes.

The promised advance had already commenced—the 1st Brigade crossing the long-looked-at Blood river, and winding slowly across the grass-land beyond. The drift over the river bore signs of having been hurried through; the sides were steep and sloppy, and the black mud in the bottom, increasing continually, threatened to swallow up each succeeding waggon. Far on the left were the Lancers, dotted about; nearer at hand, the advancing infantry, clearly marked by black lines drawn across the veldt. Beyond, again, the swells of grass-land, then yellow, reach up for some miles to a broken ridge of flat-topped hills, grass-grown to their summit; that on the left, "the Incenci" —both the "c's" pronounced hard; that on the right, Itelezi — later on a station from which the heliograph flashed its messages far on towards the front. Between these two hills is a neck, or saddle-back, yellow with the everlasting grass; and on this neck our first camp was pitched, succeeded by the more permanent erection, "Fort Warwick."

Nowhere was there a sign of life,—the country was quite deserted, save by the troops crossing. Wood's column was out of sight, ten miles further north, moving parallel with the Division. A dark object, some miles away, draws out many field-glasses, all anxious for the much-talked-of *Impi*; but it turns out to be only an over-worked ox, which has wandered so far, and now stood waiting sadly for death. Overhead the vultures soared, in horrid expectancy of their meal. In the hollow formed by the river stood groups of sentries, dark against the yellow grass in their greatcoats. Where the camp had just rested, on the Natal side of the river, were piles of stores, in every state of disorder; ranks of waggons, packed and unpacked—the officers in charge of their contents vainly trying to pick out what was wanted amongst the universal confusion; tents in rows, stretching everywhere; ambulances lumbering about; the Lancer camp, still to be known by the lances sticking up between the picket-lines, their tiny pennons fluttering gaily, as they had fluttered a hundred times before at Aldershot; staff officers galloping wildly; mule-waggons cantering merrily down the hill towards the drift; stray horses, "knee-haltered" till their noses almost touched their legs, dodging their pursuers, and refusing all attempts to catch them. In the centre of all was a substantial *laager*,—a square earthen fort, strong enough, in all conscience, and provided with two huge embrasures, red, and newly made. Our present base was but the creation of yesterday.

Following the 1st Brigade, the 2nd crossed the drift—all the heavier for the rain which fell abundantly during the night—and was at last in Zululand. A party of the 24th Regiment worked manfully at the muddy drift, shouldering the waggons, and urging the unwilling oxen across, till, after several hours, all were over, and the order came for the advance. The dry grass was knee-deep; *dongas* scored the country everywhere; small bog-holes and marshy streams crossed the track as long as it followed the low-lying meadow-land; oxen, dead or dying, were sadly plentiful. Far in front, the leading brigade was cautiously feeling its way ; then came a huge, straggling crowd of waggons, two abreast, ten abreast, drawn out for a couple of miles or more in single file,—a horrid foretaste of what was before us. But the sun shone gloriously, spirits had recovered, and the men trudged along through the grass as if the poorly-marked track across it were a turnpike-road. By the side of the column rode General Marshall, in temporary command, followed by his staff; here and there galloped in a Basuto scout, intent on something nobody could understand. The broad, well-defined road to Isandlwana was crossed, and brought up many memories; the air was full of the cracking of huge whips,—an unpleasant noise at the best of times, soon hated for its incessant continuance, under which the weary oxen, with their hides cut and seamed, winced freely. A marshy stream, not far from the ridge where we were eventually halted, caused a long delay, and it was not till the shades of night were falling around that the brigade climbed the hill and took up its ground for the night. In high quarters *"the battle of the laagers"* had been fought as was usual in those early days, every one having an opinion on the subject differing from every other, all equally effective, but quite distinct, and very perplexing to us who had to remember so many different patterns. On this first night we had three *laagers*; in the centre a huge affair, in which were accommodated the cavalry horses in long picket-lines, the Commissariat depot and issuing store-tents, and the oxen, the last countless as the sea-sand. On either side were two smaller *laagers*, one for each brigade; inside one, Lord Chelmsford and his staff—General Newdigate with his in the other. Round the outside were the tents of the regiments and the guns of the batteries; scattered about were the irregular troops, the Native Contingent, the lines of mounted corps, hospital tents, cooking-fires—a heterogeneous mass, a good deal mixed, too much scattered, and with but little method in its disposition. Round about, farther away, could be seen the dark groups of the sentries pacing to and fro. Above us rose the grand Itelezi Hill, grey and indistinct in the increasing darkness, its side scored by a great ravine, a capital hiding-place for an enemy, and so watched accordingly. In the rear, as in front, the swells of grass-land rose interminably, alive even yet with toiling waggons, cavalry horses returning from water; the background filled in with flat-topped hills, those above Dundee, left long ago, amongst them. Soldiers in every stage of untidiness wandered about the camp in that aimless way so peculiar to the race. Natives fully armed with shields and assegais continually arrived, going they never seemed to know where. Basuto horsemen chanted their evening hymn, standing in a circle, their hats off, their hands clasped tight; close by, the General, sitting on a stone, and talking over to-morrow's doings with some half-a-dozen of his staff.

Now and then the quiet was broken in upon by a shout and the noise of many men rushing, and half the camp would appear crowding frantically after two or three figures coming towards the General's tent. They were only Zulus, either real or suspected as such, who had come across the patrols, and were brought in for examination. After each wretch followed the crowd of men, struggling and pushing, intent only on satisfying their silly and childish curiosity at any cost. Indeed, the state of stupid excitement and actual nervousness to which the men had been worked up by repeated scares and continual delays, was sad, and almost hopeless. To excite curiosity, and to take advantage of the confusion it caused, we had been told, was a common Zulu stratagem, and so had to be repressed—almost an impossibility when unreasoning panic has seized upon a camp full of beings as young and as easily led as are our present-day soldiers.

We had settled down as well as was possible, amongst all these discomforts, and were sitting outside our tents before night fell and we got between the blankets, talking much, wondering much, and anticipating everything or anything, when of a sudden arose one of those undefined rumours of ill, coming no one knew whence, no one knew how. Laughter was hushed, and men's tongues stopped as their owners wandered from tent to tent seeking out the cause. And as the news leaked out, and it was whispered about that the Prince had been killed in a *kraal* close by, fighting hard, it was plain on all our faces that a great calamity had happened.

A few irregulars had galloped in with ill news on their faces, and hot haste showing in their ponies' coats. Their story was soon told—one long since too well known—and not a man in camp but felt that a friend and a guest had been lost from among us. The poor young Prince, two volunteers, and their native guide gone in a few minutes close to us, yet no one near to help.

I don't think the men who returned showed much excitement; they took off their pouches and thick boots, prepared their supper, and talked all the while as if an ordinary skirmish had taken place in which one or more had gone down, perfectly fair and to be expected in such times as these. Carey's name was not mentioned; it was then not known in the army generally that the party had been accompanied by any officer except the Prince. All that came after, and made bad worse, and regrets still more poignant. The little group of four gathered by the side of a waggon, one of those forming a side of the central *laager*, and told their tale by bits and fragments as they were asked questions by the half-dozen officers standing round. Little curiosity indeed was shown; stupor and unexpressed sorrow were predominant amongst all. Many expressions of sympathy for Lord Chelmsford under this new trial were heard, and freely acquiesced in. The men's tale was short enough. The party had been fired at suddenly, and had bolted, leaving behind the Prince and two of their comrades. From the men's looks and their unmilitary style altogether, little else could have been expected. They had not been sent out to fight; the same occurrence had happened to them before, and they had been withdrawn by their commander when attacked, as was perfectly right. What experience they had learned in war agreed entirely with their own notions as civilians. Such they were, a bit of red rag round their hats, and a bandoleer of cartridges over their shoulders, the only military part of them. All else was civilian and colonial. To them princes were no better than other men, glory but an empty name, honour unknown; their day's pay, and the enjoyments —the liberal flow of "square-face " not the least of them—which it could procure, the only object they had in going the campaign. Then it became known that an English officer had been of the party, and the tone of inquiries changed; now at least we should hear a tale which we need not feel ashamed for listening to: and the feeling of relief was heightened by one coming up and saying, "Carey, poor fellow, has made a statement which is all that can be desired, except that he has laid too much blame on to his own shoulders."

It must have been close upon seven o'clock when the party returned, and the night was falling fast around, so the body must lie where it had fallen all through it,—the rough nature of the country, only partially known as yet, utterly forbidding any midnight search. But early next morning a squadron of the

17th Lancers rode off, accompanied by several of the staff and an ambulance.

A trooper—one of those who escaped—went as a guide; and after some eight miles along a ridge commanding wide views of the surrounding country, now all covered alike with the prevailing grass, took the party down a long and wide incline, at the bottom of which evidently flowed a river. Near this, to the right, the low hills drew together; there were several patches of mealies, dry and yellow, above the river-bed, and between them and it a small *kraal*. Others were scattered about pretty plentifully on the hillsides. Riding towards the *kraal* the Lancers were halted, and the officers rode on to a slight depression, which hid each horseman as he approached it. A shout in front, and we found a trooper standing in this hollow, which was a worn and grass-grown *donga*. Beside him lay a white object, stark and stiff; beyond, a little lower down, a second; and lower down still, a third—the body of the Prince, lying staring at the sky, surrounded by the poor fellows who had died with him. It was no time for sightseeing or sentiment. The body was wrapped in a blanket, and placed reverently in the ambulance; the other two were covered up with earth, and the sad procession rode slowly back to camp.

At first it was decided to bury his body where the camp was pitched, and a party was sent out to dig a grave. But other counsels soon prevailed, and it was given out that what remained of Napoleon was to be sent home as soon as possible.

A military funeral on the spot was, however, to be given, to mark the army's respect for the dead; so on the same day, in the afternoon, the troops, formed up in a hollow square, turned out to do all that British soldiers could do in honour of the brave, dead boy. Each wing of the square was formed by the infantry—a brigade on either—their commanders, with the staff, in front. Facing the *laager* in which the body lay, and which was the fourth side of the square, were the Lancers, forming the base; in front of them, General Newdigate and his staff; the men on every side, in open order, resting on their arms reversed.

When all was silent and correct, the funeral emerged from

the *laager*, headed by a detachment of artillery marching in slow time with their carbines reversed; then the gun-carriage, drawn by six black horses, on which rested the long, almost shapeless bundle which all knew too well. Over it was cast a poor tricolour flag—the best we could make out of the scanty bits of coloured calico to be obtained. As pallbearers walked six officers of the artillery, to which corps the Prince had been attached at Woolwich; immediately in rear was the Roman Catholic chaplain; then Lord Chelmsford as chief mourner, followed by his staff.

The ground was rough with ant-heaps and holes, and the carriage jolted terribly till it was stopped opposite the Lancers—the pipers of the 21st wailing out a sad funeral-dirge. Then the priest stepped out, dressed in his fine lace surplice and quaint three-cornered hat, and in low tones read the service, bowing continually, and scattering holy water. That done, the carriage moved on round the square, the troops presented arms, and the long shapeless bundle was taken away and left under a suitable guard till next morning, when it left, under escort, for England.

Among the spectators were many well-known faces. The correspondent of the 'Figaro,' in veritable tears: his mission over, there was no longer any interest to him in the campaign, and he went home to grieve—so he told us he would do between his tears. Forbes and Stanley were close together; Fripp sketching in a quiet corner, and Melton Prior doing the same opposite. At the most solemn moment of the service an energetic photographer rushed in and hid under his black cloth-covered camera, after the fashion of his race. The instrument he has planted in the very centre of the square, his own appearance being ultra-photographic and repellent. In his hot haste with the plate his hat fell off, and showed very long and very shiny hair—a feature more conspicuous than usual in an assemblage of which every man was cropped short. I venture to say no one loved that man that day, and all watched eagerly for the last glint of the fading sun to die out before he came back. But the glow fell kindly on the bundle under the tricolour, and lingered, painting the lead-coloured wheels which carried it with crimson; and so the man got his picture, and went his way contented.

Just as the body left our sight, and the men were dismissed, a rush was made in another direction — the men, let loose, scampering off pell-mell towards the novel excitement. It was only two more spies; they might be Zulus —if our redoubted foes are poor trembling wretches, undersized and half-starved. One of them, seeing me approach with a revolver slung rather prominently round my shoulder, thought his last hour had come, and made a beseeching grab at my legs. I saw them shortly after being led away, followed by full half the camp in a disgraceful state of curious excitement, then a common and disgusting feature of our young soldiers. What became of the so-called Zulus, I never heard.

Chapter Eleven
Towards Ulundi

Our advance was certainly very leisurely done. We were to have been treated to a dash on Ulundi, while in truth we crawled thither. On the first day we saw a short seven miles of Zululand, the second a trifle more, on the third we only managed four. The oxen and the waggons they dragged were at the bottom of this sluggishness; but then we had too many of them. People took too much. I saw a deal washing-stand on a waggon not far from Ulundi. It did not belong to the regular troops—they at least were cut down to the utmost; it was our colonial friends who found baggage a necessity: in whispers it went about that those higher in position might have practised what they preached. Yet with however little ground covered, it was always the same to the troops,— "early to rise and late to bed;" in that, at least, there was no alteration. Once on the move beyond our first camp on the Itelezi ridge, and Natal was no longer visible; its hills, and the remembrance of home behind them, were blotted out, and the army at once plunged into a strange land. Yellow hills, interminable swells, isolated "*kops*," were its prominent features. Desolation was written everywhere. A surface of dry grass, yellow with age, dotted with stony hillocks— "*krantzes*," as the colony calls them. Here and there a *kraal*, its rounded huts like greater ant-heaps nestling together for some evil purpose. And across the whole landscape a network of dongas, deeply scored, sharp-sided, always hard and cruel—the fingers of skeleton hands sprawling everywhere, gripping the last remnants of life out of this dead land. No sign of life, no smoke, no labourers in the mealie-fields, no villagers sitting by the wayside and gazing at the great army; dead silence —absolutely nothing more.

There was no road, hardly any track even. As the head of the column moved, the men cut a track in the yellow grass, which tossed and waved waist-high. In front it spread itself to the horizon as the sea; the wind bent it hither and thither in broad ripples; elsewhere it was as pathless as the water: in rear of the column stretched a highway, broad, and trampled flat by the soldiers' feet.

In vain we looked on all sides for the "extensive forests of large trees, amongst which yellow wood and other valuable trees are abundant," promised us in our *vade mecum*, and supplied to us all by the authorities. The forests faded into unreality, as did many other nice bits of information supplied to us by an intelligent Government, until we reached the cactus-trees which line the Umvolosi, near Ulundi: in the country passed through to get so far was not a tree, or shrub a foot high, except at one spot on the Upoko river, where stood a bush of prickly and stunted mimosa-trees, now nearly all passed away under the British axe.

In the brigade which led the way the regiment in front moved in column of companies, with a front of some fifty yards; then followed a battery, the guns two and two, in readiness to turn to either flank; lastly, the second infantry regiment, moving as did the first. Strangely-curved lines, three or four abreast, straggled behind, coiling down the sides of the swells, or creeping in sinuous zigzags up the opposite side. A rope well frayed trailing after us was a fair simile. Line upon line, coil after coil, tops the horizon in rear and wanders after us. These were the waggons on which our life depended in this desolate land, stretching for several miles amid a series of hills and ravines, in any of which, we were told, the enemy might be lurking.

At one place is a stream, with a block of waggons at the drift crossing it; the roadway trampled into mud, the water the consistency of pea-soup. On the bank stands Lord Chelmsford, working hard, much too hard, urging the ungainly oxen over, and endeavouring to put some little method into the obstinate drivers. And men passing looked at him with some astonishment, and asked one another, "Where is the staff?"

Then behind the waggons, in the far distance, grew into sight line upon line, mathematically-straight and parallel, their component parts black against the yellow grass—an array which the glasses showed to be the Lancers leading the way for the second brigade, on that day told off as the rear-guard. More of the Lancers were on advanced duty, five miles ahead of the column, their dark forms appearing now and then as they skirmished up the distant swells. Mounted Basutos, as scouts, covered the flanks, now pushing through the long grass, or cutting across *dongas* like cats, as they made a dash at some distant *kraal* where there might be Zulus or "loot."

A small "*kop*" rose out of the valley on the right, very isolated, and interesting from its associations — but of yesterday as it seemed. For it was the place where the Prince saw his first Zulus, driving them off, and ascending after the skirmish to the top. The day had been a pleasant one, and he named the little hill in fun " Napoleon's Kop." He could have seen from it the place where, not many days after, he fought and died.

Scattered about amongst the waving grass were untidy patches of cultivation, utterly crooked and irregular in shape, fenced round with stones roughly heaped up. The mealies had been gathered, their stalks alone remaining; but the Kafir corn was standing, and horses disappeared in marvellously quick time in these paradises of forage, the long stalks and heavy heads hanging from their mouths when they reappeared on the far side, their masters carrying armfuls of the same for future use.

In the far distance loomed a great flat-topped mountain, half hidden in the morning mist. This was Inlhlazatsi, the monster whose fabled horrors of bush and precipice had frightened us out of our original route. Nearer at hand is the Ingutu range, under whose shadow the Prince was killed.

On every mountain-top within sight our vedettes crept, a mounted man in front, the three others of the party following on foot, their horses led. It was indeed "feeling" for the enemy.

Then the crest of a ridge, stony in the extreme, is reached, and we look down a broad, grassy spur, perfectly open, and with a gentle incline towards the river Ityotyozi, about two miles distant. On the right the hills draw closer, their sides dotted with *kraals*, amid which our mounted scouts were foraging.

95

Mealie-patches were plentiful, and also the circles of stones in which the cattle are kept at night. Rank grass covered the face of the land, and reached well up the men's waists as they waded on towards the four lances which marked the corners of the night's *laager*. The infantry lying down when the river-bank was reached, disappeared in the grass; the cavalry off-saddled, and led their horses down to water. A few mounted men, and some stragglers on foot, moved away a hundred yards to the right, towards a small *kraal*, with its stone cattle-pen and wide circles of perfectly white grass, common in Zululand. The *kraal* was a very mean affair, I think with only five huts, small and weatherworn; the cattle-enclosure also mean, untidy, and somewhat low. All about, the grass was tall and rank, except towards the position the troops then rested in, the future camp, the circle of white grass spoken of being there, and not growing to any height at any time.

The *kraal* stood in the entrance to a valley, in which the river ran, formed by the Ingutu range on the left, and a lower and detached spur on the right partly behind the huts. Towards the river, some hundred yards from them, the ground was level, but covered with rank grass : on the right of them the slope of the hill began, gradual at first, steeper after some hundreds of yards ; and on this slope were mealie-gardens dotted, extending back up the hill, but not coming very close to the *kraal*.

So it was seen that the collection of wretched huts which composed it was surrounded on three sides, and open only on the fourth—the side pointing to the camp, and to the way it had marched from the last one. But on riding a little nearer, we came across a *donga*, shallow certainly, and much worn, but still an obstacle, and so closing up the apparently open ground on the fourth side.

It was clearly not one of those cruel, perpendicular-sided dongas already described. This was old and worn; its depth might have been ten feet; its sides sloped so as to render it perfectly easy to cross at any part; close by, a side gully ran into the main one, and made a gently sloping road into it. Grass grew down the sides and along the bottom. If a brook had run down it, any one would have seen the whole a hundred times before at home; it was wider, nothing more.

But the sight that met our eyes on that day, as we rode up to the edge, was one not seen at home, or indeed often anywhere.

In the centre stood bareheaded a group of rough, cord-coated men, with carbines across their backs, and bandoleers studded with cartridges round their chests. By their side was a clergyman in his surplice, reading the burial-service, and at their feet a few clods of earth, laid lengthways. The words of the service, strangely, suddenly heard, floated up from the *donga*, and away across the perfect stillness, and needed no "Amen." The rough-coated men were doing the last act of respect to their two comrades who died with the Prince, and lay hardly buried under the clods. When the service was finished and the men had gone, a sergeant of the Lancers, who had helped to place them there, lifted one up, the size of his fist, and there lay the white face, still in death. Lower down a foot protruded, and on the other side a shoulder was partly bare. The earth was hard, and the tools to dig it only lances. After the camp was pitched, the poor fellows got decent burial. Just in sight of these poor mounds was a pile of stones laid roughly, lengthways also, pointing up the donga, to mark the spot where we found the Prince's body only yesterday. Round about the ground was trodden, with seams of darker soil; the grass and leaves were damp with blood-stains, and the stones bore splashes of the same. There were no marks of his horse near the spot; probably he was struck fatally at the edge of the *donga*, and falling down, knew nothing more. That the first stab was fatal, was told long afterwards by the Zulus, the man who gave it being killed at Ulundi; the others merely fell upon his dead body. There was no malice in his death; the Zulus knew that he was a great "*Inkoss*," whose death would please their king; and they killed him after their custom, and sent his sword to Cetewayo.

A worse death overtook the poor native guide chosen for the task as the most trustworthy man in the Native Contingent. He must have run for a mile across the ground taken up two days afterwards by the camp, and died there fighting hard, as we found his body, where it lay, pierced with assegai-wounds, the broken weapons lying strewn about.

Some two hundred yards beyond the donga was the *kraal*, the huts torn and ripped. At the door of one crouched one of the old women left behind by the Zulus at many of their villages, hideous and ugly beyond words to describe. The dry skin hung like parchment from her bones, and she jabbered away, with many gesticulations, boasting, as our interpreter said, that it was her sons who killed the Prince.

"They killed your great *Inkoss*: they are gone now to the king's *kraal* to fight you white men. What do you come here for? We don't want you. This is Zululand. Keep to your own side!"

Lying on the floor of a hut was the Prince's shirt, stiff with blood, and pierced with assegai-stabs. In the cattle-enclosure the natives were tapping the ground with assegais to find out where the grain was buried. An officer was sitting on the wall sketching. A broken gourd, a hearth-brush, the embers at which the Zulus cooked their last meal, and some parched mealies, were lying about. It was hardly the place for the last of the Napoleons to die at; it was so mean, so poor, so abject in its dirt and poverty. As we marched away next morning, the smoke of that hideous *kraal* went up to heaven, with that of eight others round it, fired by the Basutos as their last act in that too memorable valley.

Long afterwards, reading the accounts of the occurrence in the English papers, we were much amused. One writer talked about the "river Ityotyozi cutting off retreat towards the more open ground." As a matter of fact, the ground on the far side of the river was the slope of the Ingutu range, steep and studded with *kraals*; while to make for it was to ride straight into Zululand, and directly away from our camp.

The river too, at that time of the year, was the smallest possible trickle, not an inch deep in places, winding over a broad bed of hard sand, between low and shelving banks. Another found the grass and grain round the *kraal* "formed a very close growth of a fairly uniform height of six feet." With the exception of the mealie-stalks, which were at some little distance from the huts, there was nothing anything like as high near the *kraal*, which was barely so high itself, being plainly visible from any point round.

"The Kafir probably rushed to cover at once, and was there surrounded," is a sentence which threw considerable doubts on the accuracy of the remaining portion; while the number of Zulus attacking was at first put down at from forty to fifty,—a figure gradually coming down, until the last accounts place it as actually eight, and no more.

One thing has been omitted steadily from all accounts. The advancing Zulus, seeing our men in full retreat, called after them in mockery, "Ah, you English cowards, you always run away!"

Some three miles further down the river, opposite the drift which we made and crossed on our onward way, Lord Chelmsford commenced the first fort; but there it ended—the fort was begun, a line of parapet was piled up, and a mountain of stores deposited, and that was all. It was never finished.

That afternoon Wood sent in word that his pet *Impi* was approaching—I am not sure that there were not two of them—and so *laagering-up* was the order of the day. The waggons were urged across the drift, and dragged into square on the right bank close to it with feverish haste. A battle was imminent, and so we put our best foot foremost. A message was sent to the two companies left behind on the other side, as the garrison of the contemplated fort, to rejoin at once. The commander sent back to say that the stores were lying there, and he could not leave them till waggons arrived to remove them; whereupon a peremptory order was sent back telling him to let them lie, so long as he came over with his men. He obeyed, and many waggon-loads of stores lay at any one's mercy through the night.

However, the *Impi* did not turn up—as indeed many had suggested when the report of its arrival came in—and we passed the night undisturbed. It would have been a blessing indeed if the *Impi* had appeared, and so put us out of suspense, really trying to all—the continual battling against an unseen foe, eternally on the *qui vive* for a battle which never came.

Lord Chelmsford has been blamed unjustly for his extreme caution during these early days, when the feeling which prompted it with him was equally shared by every officer in the camp. It is easy enough to fight an enemy in the open; but to be ever on the watch for one unknown, unseen, is a trial which few can realise until they have experience of its influence on men's spirits. Very early the next morning the cavalry turned out in search of the *Impi*, followed at daylight by the guns and infantry.

The air was alive with light; sunshine sat and shimmered on the white quartz-reefs which cropped out every here and there. In front, a solitary thorn-tree was a feature in the landscape, as being the first seen in Zululand; beyond were the mountains enclosing the Umvolosi river, bare and precipitous, seemingly impenetrable. The smoke of burning *kraals* rose in blue columns from the valley. Groups of Basuto horsemen crowned the hills, a stray figure here and there separated from the rest, circling round the huts to which he had just set fire. A mile farther, and a fresh valley, shaped like a basin, lies in front; across this, and up its opposite slopes, streamed Wood's column. In the centre winds a new river, the Nonchoini, soon to be dominated by the Gatlings in Fort Newdigate on its banks. Along these now stretch innumerable dongas. Between them a few *kraals* are sending up their smoke to heaven. There are no other signs of life save these in that great valley.

But hope ran high that morning as the column was leisurely crossing the Nonchoini, a message coming from Lord Chelmsford in front to say that an action had commenced. At once faces brightened as General Newdigate, riding in front of a neat blue and white flag, hastened the brigade across the drift into position on the crest of one of the great folds which seemed ever to rise in front of us as we toiled over them. Swords were loosened and their knots unwound, revolvers examined, and every officer coming from the front anxiously questioned.

Some declared that they heard firing.

Just then a group of savage-looking fellows were brought in and halted in front of the General. There were nine of them,— four elderly men, with long grave faces, their heads topped by the black ring denoting a married man ; the rest younger, some mere boys, more savage and unkempt than the first. One truculent savage had his hair tousled into little soppets, glistening with fat, and grimed with dirt. On his forehead was a recent assegai-wound. They sported as clothes a dirty brown blanket apiece, and were as forbidding and unpleasant a lot to look at as one could wish for. By their side lay a bundle of dry sheepskins, which moved spasmodically, and at length induced some one looking on to cut the bit of hide which bound them together, when out rolled an old woman, hideously bony, and at death's door from old age and starvation.

The old men proved to be ambassadors sent by Cetewayo to ask for terms; the young ones were the servants; the old hag no one owned. These were the messengers who went to Crealock on the Tugela, and were sent on to Lord Chelmsford as the proper person with whom to treat. They looked sulky enough, and their evil looks did not grow more pleasant when a guard was marched up and rattled on their bayonets with an ugly clatter.

"What do you English want here?" they growled. "We don't want you; go away! We want to be friends with such great people. Tell us what you want, and go away!"

The fellows were subsequently put up for the night in the *laager* just opposite Lord Chelmsford's tent, and entertained royally with "*scoff*;" but their ill-looks remained unchanged by our hospitality. The *Graphic* made an excellent sketch of one or two of the principal men, which afterwards appeared in the paper. Small groups of officers surrounded them, talking when it was possible through an interpreter; but the expression of their faces never changed—they scowled on, and looked ready for murder and bloodshed at any moment.

The idea was to show them the glory of the invading army, and then let them go to carry their tale home—a mistaken estimate of the Zulu character altogether. They scowled at us impertinently during their stay; were but little impressed by the sight of the half-grown boys who loafed round them as English warriors; got an excellent view of the interior arrangements of our *laager*, with the position of the General's tent to an inch; and carried off our impossible terms of peace, together with a fine fat ox as a present. It was not a bad day's work altogether. The fight in front turned out to be a skirmish between our cavalry and some thousand or more of the villagers who lived round about Ibabanango, and naturally objected to our destructive propensities. It was the day poor Frith of the 17th Lancers was shot dead off his horse, potted from the bushes on a hillside, in a place where no horse could go, the last which cavalry should attack.

However, it was done; the correspondents, as usual, being the first to return into camp with the news—after them, in a cloud of dust, the 17th and King's Dragoon Guards. They rode along in sections, two abreast, their pennons torn and draggled, the men sitting erect, and the horses not half done up. In rear came an ambulance with Frith's body.

He was buried that evening in an old mealie-field, by the side of a brook below the camp, Lord Chelmsford and most of the officers attending. Round his grave a single rank of Lancers presented their lances as the body was lowered. Here, as elsewhere, were no volleys fired. In the dim light the uniforms were blended into one grey mass, hardly to be distinguished one from another; and the service, with "Our Father" repeated reverently by the little group of soldiers, sounded strangely solemn and peaceful after the bustle of the camp.

Chapter Twelve
Alarm!

Night fell as the funeral-party returned; and I was lying snugly in bed—two blankets and a waterproof sheet laid out on some charming specimens of quartz—having further indulged in taking off my boots, in anticipation of a good night's rest, when *ping! ping! ping!* went three shots, the signal of an attack.

In an instant the drowsy camp awoke as if by magic. The Native Contingent crowded into the *laager*, buzzing like bees. Our own men raced each other, in a hurry to be first within welcome cover. The bugles rang out the "assembly," a weird sound; between the pauses were heard the words of command. Flop came the tent about my ears, and I was outside in the darkness. The air was full of the noise of hurry and bustle. Confusion put in its own voice, and was heard. From a rift in the clouds a streak of light fell on the heads of silent men in the waggons peering out, and gave promise of the rising moon. Here and there flashed a bayonet, pointing outwards. Inside the waggons was a space, ten yards across, left vacant for a roadway, and within this lay the vast crowd of oxen, tied by the head, and breathing noisily. Between them, here and there, were the horses, picketed in lines, straining nervously at their head-ropes; the men beside their horses, in readiness to mount.

At that moment came a volley far down the hill where a picket had been posted, its rattle clear and distinct in the night air. A staff officer gallops past; and in an instant the rear face is lit up with fire, taken up all along the line of waggons. Crash go the volleys everywhere, belching out flame and smoke, till the front is one thick white cloud, pierced only by the sharp and vivid flashes from the muzzles.

"*Whisht*" comes a bullet overhead. "*Whir!*" follows another after. Crash goes a volley close by, and the face in our front is once more framed with fire. Then the big guns in the corner give out an answer, booming their bass notes high above the rest. The bullets are flying merrily overhead ; and the soldiers, young lads half of them, with a wholesome dread of the Zulus in their poor little hearts, and funk plainly written on their faces, crowd under the waggons for safety, quickly to be pulled out again by their officers in every style of undress, many with their red nightcaps still on. Out come the skulkers in droves, only to vanish again round the next waggon. The fun grows furious. Bullets sing and whiz past in flights. The smoke is stifling, and hides up everything. Half-a-dozen horses, maddened by the din, are rushing about. In the narrow pathway left round the waggons it is impossible to move freely, so crowded up is it with oxen and horses. Native soldiers squat in masses in the middle, and continually let off their guns in the air, keeping the butts firmly on the ground. Conductors blaze away into the nearest waggon-tilt. Tents lie flat, their ropes still tied to the pegs, sure traps for the unwary. Chaos is everywhere, even in the waggons, where the men lie, firing incessantly, and paying but scant attention to the orders shouted at them.

Twenty minutes of this work, and a bugle sounds the "cease fire," and the flashes die out and leave the *laager* dark and silent as the night itself.

Then our General followed, and gave his censure pretty freely on the wretched scare; and shame sat on many a face at its recollection. Not a Zulu had been seen—the picket who commenced the row firing at what it thought was some "blacks," but might have been a cloud.

It was said afterwards, by the Zulus themselves, that there were 15,000 of them ready to attack, but gave it up on finding us so well prepared. The tale may be true or not, and was some small consolation to those who helped in the fun, though hardly so to the wounded men on our own side, shot by their comrades, who were picked up after the firing ceased.

From that day, the spot where the scare happened was called, in memory of it, "Fort Funk."

Amusing sights there were. Men in every stage of undress left their tents and bolted for the waggons. I saw one of our parsons struggle out of his tent as it fell, his only dress his shirt, a bundle of clothes in one hand, his boots and revolver in the other, and make for the shelter-trench, already bristling with bayonets. Here he missed his seat on a mealie-bag, and tumbled backwards on to the broad of his back. But matters at such times are too serious for joking, and so the occurrence gained but small notice.

If ever there was a war of "fatigues," the Zulu war was that one. The constant loading and unloading of waggons; the dragging the heavy machines into *laager*, not unfrequently altered after finished at every camping-ground ; the eternal digging and trenching in ground often solid as stone itself; the tree-felling with axes that were soft and notched, and the piling them into waggons horrent with thorns of previous loads; the coal-getting, mealie-gathering, and last, and most distasteful of all, the collection of cow-dung, to supplement our scanty supply of fuel,—all were wearisome and ever-recurring sorts of "fatigues."

The day after our scare at Fort Funk we moved on about nine miles, and camped on the banks of the Upoko river, a spot the most picturesque yet seen. We were told that it was a favourite resort of Cetewayo's in the hot weather, owing to the trees and constant water-supply. It is, moreover, the headquarters of Sirayo, his most devoted follower, and at the same time one most hostile to the English—his sons having brought about proximately the present state of affairs by the seizure of a wretched woman in Natal territory on some pretence not admitted by the Government.

The camp was pitched on a somewhat steep slope towards the river, which was little else but a trickle over sand and stones some half-mile distant. Beyond it was the great mass of Ibabanango,—a vast assemblage of flat-topped hills, split in all directions by valleys, above which the rounded top of the central mountain lifted up, and pointed to our onward way. The base of the hills was scored by terrible-looking dongas, stretching in every direction, deep and impassable. Their sides were somewhat thickly wooded by mimosa-bushes, *kraals* hid away between them. Mealie-fields were abundant. Four waggons taken at Isandlwana stood in a *kraal* nearly in front of us, their woodwork perfect, the paint as bright a green as the day they were lost. Near these was a patch of herbage dirtier than the ever-present grass—the field of mealies in which Frith was shot.

Everywhere were caves and holes cunningly hidden in the sides of the *dongas*, and amongst them our native allies were busy. Isandlwana relics were abundant. Martini cartridges ripped open to get at the powder; a new saddle and saddle-bags complete; rifles of 24th and 80th Regiments; soldiers' valises; a gunner's oil-bottle; a pair of ammunition-boots; a pearl-handled knife; a cake of soap and a sponge, the last two very puzzling to the possessors. In one of these burrows six ill-looking Kafirs were caught, and only just saved their lives, on its being proved that they were drivers in our own camp. This was an event which showed plainly the ease with which the Zulus obtained information of our doings: the men taken, if not actual spies, were quite ready to turn their knowledge to account if captured by the enemy.

On the day of our arrival at the Upoko, a man on a white horse, put down as Sirayo himself, gathered the people of the district, the same who on the previous day had fired on our cavalry, and brought some thousands of them boldly down to the drift which led to our advancing column. On seeing them, Lord Chelmsford sent back for a couple of guns, which at once opened fire on the Zulus. The first shot fell short, and did not stop them ; at the second they hesitated; the third dropping in the middle of them, turned the whole lot, and made them bolt to a man. The last we saw of them, they were swarming up the grassy spurs of the hill in rear of their *kraals*, like ants in a hurry.

The country was subsequently overhauled by the first brigade and some cavalry, and the whole nest of them cleared away. Their *kraals*, after being burnt, were searched for buried grain, which is stored in holes dug here and there in the cattle-pens. The holes are neatly made, some eight feet in depth, shaped like jars, with a narrow neck, the opening just large enough to admit a boy. The inside is carefully plastered, and the mealies being poured in, the orifice is closed with a flat stone, strewn with earth and manure to escape observation; and it was one of the curious sights of the campaign to watch "Tommy Atkins" poking about gravely with his bayonet up to the hilt in cow-dung. It happened to be Trinity Sunday when this was being done. On the right, Buller's Horse were feeling their way up a valley, leaving behind them columns of smoke, the marks where *kraals* had been. On the left were the 17th advancing in troops across a ridge, flanked by the guns of a battery, the shells bursting against the side of the mountain in puffs of smoke; burning *kraals* on that side also. In front of the *laager*, on the slope which led to the river, beyond which the panorama was spread, were the troops of the second brigade, formed into a square for church service. Near at hand was a smaller body standing uncovered in front of a tent in which the Roman Catholic priest was praying before a temporary altar, gay with red velvet and brass candlesticks; while behind, again, a lesser group still was chanting a hymn Wesleyans led by their own minister in plain clothes.

In front, fire and death; far away, great Inlhlazatsi; nearer, and to our left, Ibabanango, its summit just showing above the level hill-tops at its base; then the steep-sided Isipezi, and the sharp peak of Alarm Hill, from either of which Isandlwana is plainly visible: such were our surroundings on that Sunday morning.

Everywhere the same sea of dry grass, broken only by quartz-reefs and piles of boulders. A ghastly land, where life was just possible, sustained on milk and mealie-meal. Not a fruit-tree in the land save at the few missionaries' gardens. Even the banana, ever present, is not there; wild-flowers here and there in patches; a few birds, songless altogether; just life, and nothing more.

The people want little more than guns, and cattle with which to purchase wives. Clothing is not wanted among people who go naked. Books are useless with a nation whose language is unwritten. Wealth was their almost certain death. The king heard of a subject who owned a hundred cattle more than the rest. That night an *Impi* was at his *kraal*, and surrounded it. A signal was given, and the huts were fired; the wretches flying from the flames were met by the assegais of the soldiers, and stabbed to death. Not one escaped. Men, women, children, and live things, even the dogs, were killed; and the work was only finished when the silence of death was over the accursed spot. Then the warriors returned to the king with the cattle they had taken, and departed to their own *kraals*, only to be in turn the victims of his will. Hence arose the custom, common in Cetewayo's day, for the headman of a village every night of his life to "sleep in the grass" —in other words, to hide away from his own house at nights.

Our camp on the Upoko was the scene of fresh delay, and consequent discontent. Wood's column, supplemented by a portion of the Division, was sent back to Natal for more supplies, and streamed past on its backward road as Lord Chelmsford moved towards that position. The two columns meeting presented a remarkable and strange appearance. Regiments, mixed up with the everlasting waggons, moved separately; natives were everywhere; in Wood's column the bands were playing lively tunes, waking up the silence, and rendering matters a little less dismal: on all sides was a vast crowd, seemingly without any approach to order; yet on arrival in camp every one settled down into the place allotted.

While this force was absent, extra precautions against attack were taken with the Division, it being naturally thought that the enemy would take advantage of the divided army. The *laager* was strongly trenched, and dynamite placed under the rocks which commanded it, each charge connected with a battery in the camp.

Native spies, too, were freely used. Three of them were induced to start on this somewhat ticklish service, the preparations being first a feed, when each put away some seven pounds of beef. In the evening they were ready to start, doing so with much show, and making for a spot at some distance from the camp, where they took off what clothes they had, and hid them away in an ant-bear's hole. Then followed a coat of grease to prevent capture, and the preliminaries were completed. Usually they made for some hill, selecting a place on its summit where they can hide in tolerable safety, and from which the country to be watched can be well observed. This found, they stay there for a couple of days, descending the third night, and making for the camp with any news they have gathered. Should they fall in with the Zulus, they have been coached up in their replies — their guns came from Isandlwana, where they fought in the ranks of the Inbube or the Udududu regiment; they have the names of the officers of these off pat, with other like general information, being careful to mention those corps only which are recruited in distant parts of the country. With all their adroitness, they were apt to be assegaied now and then when detected; the great thing in their favour being that, native-like, they are the most consummate liars. So much so are they, that it was often more than doubtful whether the whole story of their adventures was not a fresh example of their natural abilities.

By some of them the Intabankulu Mountain, some twenty-five miles north of the camp, was reported to be alive with Zulus and their cattle; and Buller started off for it on a two days' trip with the Irregulars across the *donga*-intersected valley between. There was little resistance shown; his arrival was sudden and unexpected, and he was able to burn many villages, and drive off some three or four hundred cattle without much trouble. The cattle were mostly cows and calves, pretty little animals, with soft eyes and gentle ways, much too good for so savage a people. Amongst them were a few of the trek-oxen taken at Isandlwana — huge, gaunt beasts, that had not fared over-well since their capture. The lowing of the herd was deafening, the confusion being helped by servants from the camp picking out milch-cows for their masters. Most of the cows had a grass rope run through their nose, the ends tied tightly round the animal's horns—a method, we were told, of taming them.

It was in this camp that the court-martial ordered for the trial of Carey was sitting. A marquee belonging to the Commissariat had been pitched in the passage at one end of the *laager*, between the waggons and a row of officers' tents; and to it was the unfortunate man led daily by the officer in whose charge he had been placed. A few officers—not many—interested in the case, attended the court, but there was little excitement evinced; still less when the proceedings terminated, and it was whispered abroad that the sentence had been adverse to the prisoner, and terribly severe. It was not a pleasant matter to talk about, and was banished from men's thoughts as much as possible.

More amusing topics were those told about our recent scare at Fort Funk. One, that a quartermaster of one of the regiments engaged, was seen going among the men, rubbing his hands with delight, and crying out, "Fire away, boys! fire away! Give it to them hot, lads! There's lots more ammunition out here when that's done."

Hard by, a lancer who had been outside when the alarm was given, was squeezing his body between two waggons in his hurry to join his comrades, when a squad of them, catching sight of him suddenly in that position, took him for one of the enemy, and fired full at him, crying out, "Here they come, boys! here's the Zulus a-creeping through! blaze away at 'em, my beauties!" And blaze away they did, and brought him down with a bullet in his neck.

Camp "shaves" were numerous, and passed the unwelcome delay after a fashion.

"Catchwayo," as the soldiers call him, hearing that some of his *kraals* had been burnt, had sent an Induna with 40,000 men to form the president and members of a court of inquiry which was to sit and investigate the matter. So well was this put about that the day of the arrival of the court was mentioned, and I overheard two men talking about it just as though it had been published as a fact in "regimental orders."

"Parade's at ten o'clock, aint it, Jim?"

"Is it? I didn't hear of it. What's it been changed for?"

"Why, of course—haven't you heard? —because the enemy's expecting!"

Fifteen dead Zulus were said to have been found in a *kraal*, killed by one shell. On doubts being raised as to the truth of the story, a man is ready at once with an authentic narrative. "I saw

110

the niggers creeping inside, myself, about two dozen of them; then the shell bursted among the lot, and I never seen one of 'em come out again" — an excellent specimen of eyesight, as the range on that day was a little over a mile, at which distance a Zulu on all-fours, in grass over his head, is no easy object to distinguish.

The Native Contingent, being armed with muzzle-loaders, got leave now and then to fire off their rifles to prevent the charge getting too old for use. It happened that on one of these occasions an officer of comfortable proportions had gone down to the river to bathe, and was disporting himself in a pool when the volley went off. Not having been warned, and thinking it was the long-expected Zulu attack, the bather sprang up the bank, revolver in hand, and made full speed for the *laager*, before which he arrived breathless and without a scrap of clothing, amid the roars of those who caught sight of him.

Our own dress was about this time rather miscellaneous. Wardrobes calculated to last for a couple of months, must look a little seedy after nearly double that time. Sun, dust, and rain are no dress-improvers. Sleeping constantly in clothes does not renew the polish. The result is rags—rags supplemented by "slops" bought in the colony. I have already mentioned the stock article of clothing there—a hideous, snuff-coloured cord, made up into breeches or trousers, the former for choice; and it was to these that many had to be reduced. I saw a colonel in a pair of most atrocious red-brown, shining corduroys, the upper part of which was enlarged by a piece of "gunny-bag" let in. A youngster fresh from Christ Church had rigged himself out in a pair of the same of a weak coffee-mixture colour, matching most queerly the scarlet of his jacket. One general affected a blue pilot-coat with brass buttons, and looked not unlike the captain of a penny-steamboat on the Thames. Boots were a strong point. The cavalry wear riding-boots open at the instep, and lacing with a neat cross-work of leather; colonials affect high boots cut down the length of the sides, and fastening with many straps and buckles; while infantry officers had gone in for heavy double soles, studded over with nails such as are met with on the doors of our county jails.

Prices were steadily on the rise. A bottle of "square-face" fetched twenty-five shillings; while a considerable number of those addicted to it spent much time vainly hunting up a youth popularly supposed to have a case of it for sale for as many pounds. An empty bottle was worth one shilling; why, I can't say, except it was on the chance of its owner being able to refill it. A box of matches went at the same figure, and men were content to sit in the dark rather than waste one of the precious little things. Jam was steadily disappearing —a strange thing to ask for in such times, but nothing, nevertheless, so relished. A pot to finish dinner, and the tough ration-beef and greasy suet-pudding were eatable, and almost passable.

But our delay at length came to an end: Wood's column once more appeared, and passed us, going some miles farther on, as was his privilege, much to the disgust of the Division; and at last we were again on the move behind him.

We climb a hill, and cross the Upoko at a wide drift. Then the road turns eastwards and crosses a patch of ground hideous and black from the effects of a recent grass-fire. Northwards rises the huge mass of Ibabanango, held up by its company of flat-topped hills, miles broad. Eastwards is the valley of the Umlatozi, a river springing from the hills round Ibabanango, and lower down one of the main streams of the land. Behind are the hills of Natal, Isandlwana in the middle distance. Everywhere dark mountains and veldt scored with dongas. Over all rests a horrid sameness of form and colour. There are no fields, no kraals; a land deserted,—a land where the streams disappear in sand and stones; where the rivers, far between, are hidden by vast folds, to which the term of valley would be misapplied: just dry land, very dry and stony; over all a mantle of yellow grass, brown here, grey there, black where fire has burnt it up. Such is Zululand, and such: it was as our advancing camp, hardly a dot on the great panorama, rested each night on the sides of its hills—alone, lonely, desolate; nothing but itself, its tents, its waggons, its cooking-fires in long rows, and its anxious-looking tenants ever ready for a scare.

Chapter Thirteen
Battle

Opposite the drift by which the Upoko was crossed, Fort Marshall was placed. It was the third fort on the line to the rear, considerably larger than the rest, and having far more importance from its position at the junction of the roads leading to Ulundi from Rorke's Drift and Koppie Allein. It also commanded the extensive and turbulent district round Mount Ibabanango on one side, and the Qudeni bush on the other. The fort consisted of two redoubts connected by a shelter-trench, the whole dug out of the hard, solid earth, and faced with large stones. The largest redoubt was intended as a final resort should the garrison be worsted while holding the smaller one and the line of shelter-trench, and contained a couple of guns on platforms peeping over the parapet at the angles towards the river, the hospital, spare ammunition, and seven days' preserved-meat, called officially " the iron ration." Down the centre of the space enclosed by the shelter-trench was a double row of stores, bags of oats, of mealies, of sugar, of biscuit, of salt, with boxes of tea, coffee, milk, and all kinds of tinned provisions— the whole forming a depot from which to supply the army. Outside were the tents of the garrison, consisting of the detachment of artillery; a squadron of Lancers; four companies, reduced almost immediately to two, of the 21st; some native horse; and a company of the Native Contingent, their roughly-made *kraals* straggling down the hill towards a tiny stream.

On the first night of occupation, when the parapets were simply marked out on the turf, the usual scare took place, though the Division was within half a mile. It was about nine at night, when a noise of men running silently disturbed us in our first nap; the unwonted sound was taken up in an instant by the troops, who bolted out of their tents and made a rush for the line of sods which marked the position of the future fort. Out tumbled the officers in wonder: no order had been given, no sound had been heard; the men had just scuttled like frightened sheep into what cover there was. The picket declared afterwards they had heard a shot, and at once bolted to a man, the rest in the tents following in a blind, aimless way, most startling—a result of the state of nervousness to which the men had been educated.

Now any one who can realise the feelings of an English jelly-fish when left high and dry by the receding tide, can in some degree enter into my own as I found I had to remain behind for a time at this half-way house, and watch the Division wind up the slopes of Ibabanango and disappear over the crest of the last spur. It was indeed a campaign of disappointments, of leaving behind; and when we did arrive at Ulundi, those so left in rear must have more than outnumbered those who did battle with the Zulus. To leave a comfortable home, and sail some seven thousand miles, only to be left out in the cold at some cheerless, unexciting spot, is a fate not calculated to elevate the spirits; and bitter were the growls which so much of it gave rise to.

The situation of Fort Marshall was depressing and depressed. It lay in a basin. All round, the sky-line was high overhead. The sun shone on the rim of the bowl in which it was built fully half an hour before he warmed up the garrison, the damp, limp mass of tea-leaves in the bottom. On three sides was a rugged donga, impassable save at the pathways, its sides scored into a hundred chasms, through which trickled the water of many tiny streams. Quartz-reefs crop out of the grass. Fragments of coloured marbles strew the slopes. Buttresses of sandstone, snow-white, enclose the river. Rockeries of quartz are piled about, planted with strange-leaved plants, out of which spring orange and flame coloured flowers. Isipezi and Alarm Hill are behind. In the hollow near the fort the Zulu army collected for Isandlwana, and the way the columns marched lay on either side of the former. Now the garrison of the fort were, with the vultures, the only live things visible. Black patches, ever taken by nervous men for an Impi advancing, mark the dongas. A krantz spotted with scrub near the river attracts the eye, grateful for any relief from the prevailing yellow. Oxen left behind by the column stood in melancholy attitudes around. On the slopes above them the great grey vultures sat in watchful expectancy. The cattle belonging to the post were browsing in a mealie-field, beside what was once a *kraal*. Now the mealie-field, and the stone cattle-pen near it, were all that remained.

The circular patch of sky above the basin was usually blue; towards evening thunder-clouds rolled up, and distant lightning played along the sky-line. In early mornings Inthlabaumkosi caught the first rays, and glowed with fire as from a furnace-door just opposite and opened suddenly. The distant range was lit with reflected light, rose-coloured. In the centre, by some strange freak, Isipezi was alone in shadow. The morning air was biting, and the soldiers, leaning against the parapet between their bayonets, were glad of their hot coffee while waiting for daylight. It was their only solace in those long, dark mornings— not quite a thing of joy to remember, even when tempered with hot coffee. One of the saddest sights amongst us was the condition of many of the horses of the Lancers; too many, indeed, now but the framework of the animals which landed in such excellent condition at Durban two months previously. The work was hard and continuous, mostly saddle, the men spending hours there without dismounting: besides the actual cavalry work were escorts—cut down later on by an order, post-carriers—convoys, vedettes, raids, and scouting. All well enough for horses used to a colonial life, but doubly trying to those used to warm stables, excessive grooming, and good English oats and hay, represented in those times by mealies, to which they were unaccustomed, mouldy oats, and compressed-hay chaff. And rations of these were cut down as we advanced, I remember a trooper passing the troops drawn up for church service one Sunday morning riding his own and leading a second horse to water. Fifty yards beyond the square, the latter tucked his legs under him and lay down, dying where he lay, too weak to struggle.

Expeditions to reconnoitre the country formed a pleasant change from the dull daily routine, with its ever-repeated sameness in urging waggons up the stiffest of hills, expecting news of the pet *Impi* from each approaching horseman, and winding up the day with the good old *laager*. On either hand the country is traversed by valleys, divided again by hills, each capable of hiding any quantity of Zulus; and the reconnaissance has for its object to sweep these nooks, to destroy any *kraals* left unburnt, and which are used to harbour the enemy during the night, while a general idea of the lay of the land is obtained.

It was a pretty sight when one of these parties left camp of an early morning. They were often accompanied by natives on foot, found very useful as scouts; and the red coats of these, far in front and scattered freely, as is the habit of the African, contrasted well with the handsome uniform of the Lancers behind. In the distance ahead ride the scouts, dark against the sky-line.

We usually struck one of the numerous native tracks, and advanced along it in the required direction, thus getting over the dongas, up hillsides literally paved with boulders, or across tracts of grass as high as the riders' heads. The flat-topped mountains were excellent landmarks, though apt to be hidden at times by the ground. There was actually no flat; rocky spurs fall away suddenly into valleys walled in with precipices. In the centre sprawled the inevitable donga. Here and there in out-of-the-way corners were patches of cultivation, scattered about in an aimless, irregular way, making us, who were used to fields and hedgerows, wonder whether the Zulus had not gone out of their way through sheer devilment.

Near such patches usually appeared the dome-shaped huts, white with exposure, and surrounded with dirt and rubbish. The pattern is invariable; the sites chosen, to an Englishman, inexplicable. Fat valleys abounding with pasture and running water are neglected for a gaunt hillside, half-way up which a rocky shelf just affords space for the *kraal*. Below will be a labyrinth of dongas, above the crags of a rock-terrace, both equally impassable. These sites, moreover, are cunningly contrived. You see a *kraal* a couple of miles across the valley, and think an easy ride will take you to it. If a native is told to take you, the chances are that he starts in a direction totally opposite to where it appears; the ride after him will probably consume an hour or more; some two or three valleys, each with its own pet system of dongas, will be met with ; while, stranger still, the *kraal* itself will vanish before you have gone a hundred yards, and you will only find it again when of a sudden it pops up under your very nose, not ten yards in front of it.

In the centre will be the *cattle-kraal*, its floor trampled hard by cattle, its entrance closed by logs, forked so as to be able to hold up a bar; and round this will be the huts, their openings invariably pointing inwards towards the *cattle-kraal*, those of the more pretentious inhabitants surrounded by a screen of mats. Mats are a specialite of the Zulus. I saw some made out of grass, something like lavender in scent and colour; the flowers were left on the stems, and woven in so as to form a silver-grey lining to the mat. These are used principally as the wardrobes in which the men's cowtail dresses and other finery are kept. These are again rolled up and enclosed in a log hollowed out, the only clothes-press of these queer people.

Round the *kraal* the earth is trodden hard, swept and tidy; but alongside are trails of rank grass, piles of refuse, half-gnawed bones, and broken pots. Inside is utter darkness, till your eyes grow accustomed to the light, or rather want of it. You then see the floor is beaten hard with cement, mud, or cow-dung principally; there is no furniture, only a few mats, and perhaps a Kafir pillow—a bit of wood quaintly shaped about two feet in length, supported on three carved legs. In the centre is the fireplace —a circle of pebbles an inch or two above the floor. The wicker frame of the hut is black with smoke and dirt; flies and cockroaches come out in armies; fleas disport themselves in their own happy way. Hollow gourds of strange shapes lie about; baskets, closely woven, contained once beer or milk; earthen pots, beautiful ovals, and thinner than our home manufacture, are for boiling. A number of dogs, homeless and hungry, peer in at the unwonted intruders, and howl out their disappointment at finding them white. Then a match is applied to the weather side of a hut, and the dry mats crackle and blaze up high and

117

fierce; the smoke rises in dense columns from each hut fired in succession, and in a few minutes the *kraal* is but so many glowing cones of red-hot fire. Soon the grass catches, and the flames run along the ground with great rapidity, licking up the smaller patches, roaring and crackling through the mealie-fields, leaping dongas, sweeping up the opposite hill, and creeping through the boulders which form the battlements of the cliff above. A shout is heard from the rocks farther away, and the natives are seen waving aloft the spoil which they have found hidden away in them. Mats, guns, dresses, gourds, pillows, Isandlwana loot, everything which a Zulu thinks worth hiding, is there, and quickly hauled out, and packed away on the spoilers' backs for sale hereafter in camp. Far away the fire is galloping across the *veldt*, with a front increasing every minute; night alone will quench its fury. The huts have fallen in, and lie so many heaps of smoking ashes. The work of destruction is complete, and the party ride away towards the next valley.

One day a second party of ambassadors from Cetewayo came in—seven of them—big-limbed, broad-shouldered fellows, with long grave faces, somewhat Jewish in cast, and a cruel look in their eyes, always restless and on the watch. A blanket is the dress of the chiefs; the servants, good-looking youths, with only the "*moucha*" round their middles, sit apparently unconscious of all around them, quite content to shoulder their bundles at a look from their masters. These carry a letter in a cleft stick, and evidently look upon it as a precious safeguard, presenting it to any one who approaches with the usual salute, "*Koss*" (chief), accompanied by raising a hand or finger above the head.

The despatch turned out to be the letter mentioned in the Dutchman's account of Cetewayo, and his captivity with him, which appeared some months afterwards in the *Daily Telegraph*. It was wrapped in a dirty bit of waterproof, suspiciously like a piece from an officer's overcoat, and was written in pencil on a blank page of an old account-book, ruled for accounts in red ink. It was the usual rigmarole,—"Why did we come? why had we burnt my *kraals*? Go backwards, and send Shepstone and your Governor of Natal to talk to me." As it was nearly night, and too late to send them through our sentries to Lord Chelmsford, who was some distance ahead, they were provided with a tent for the night, and a guard—as much for their own safety as our own. About nine o'clock that night, just as the camp was in its first sleep, a man of this guard came up breathless with nervous funk, knocked up the officer in charge, and burst out with the intelligence, "If you please, sir, them blacks is sharpening their assegais inside their tent, and we think it is not safe unless there is more of us to look after them." It turned out that the half-famished Zulus were trying to eat their dinners; the tent was without a light, and the "sharpening of assegais" was the clatter of their cooking-pans.

On one of these days the mail arrived, bringing a few newspapers, which were a great treat. Amongst them a magazine, in which occurred some lines on Isandlwana by Robert Buchanan, and which put the whole camp into roars of laughter: the sentiment expressed was so truly wonderful, the poetical licence so unchecked; while our mirth was not a little helped by the delightful comments of a weekly paper. It was something like this—

"Oh listen to that warning cry,
'Fly, British soldiers, fly,
For the dusky foe is nigh
From Isandula!'"

What little time we had to ourselves was occupied in eating and sleeping, with bits of conversation mixed up here and there. In this last the hateful *laager* was a continual subject of animadversion. Only let us meet them in the open, shoulder to shoulder, and we could lick the Zulus as we have licked better people before. Open order or skirmishing was equally bad the other way; adopt those tactics, and the Zulus will lick us. But to run behind a waggon at every alarm was childish, and rankled deep in our hearts. Yet the lessons, by continual repetition, had their effect on many; and I have heard men say that it would be a matter of impossibility to hold a line of shelter-trench, such as we made at Fort Marshall, even when it was flanked, as that was, by the fire crossing its face from redoubts at either extremity.

As to eating, beef—everlasting beef—was our sole support. We got to hate the sight of an ox. All day we had to witness his invincible dislike to go with us in the waggons; and every night we had to see him again, boiled, roasted, or stewed, for dinner. We baked him in pies, we boiled him in pudding, we chopped him fine as mince, we mixed him in stews; but all with the same result. The ox revenged his sufferings on us even when cut into steak.

No wonder one's thoughts turned sometimes to the dinners we should order when we got home again. Alas! when our anticipations would be realised, our appetites would no longer remain as they were then. Of all things provocative of a good dinner, the Zulu air was the best; pity 'twas we got so much of it, while obtaining so little with which to satisfy its demands.

Meanwhile the column crept on slowly towards the king's *kraal*. The native road thither branched off to the left of our own soon after leaving Fort Marshall, and wound over the northern slopes of Ibabanango, while we followed the southern, soon leaving them altogether. This Zulu road was worn and trampled into many ruts and holes, and was some fifty feet in width, crossing the most impossible *dongas*, and climbing the steepest hills, intent only on finding the nearest cut. It was of course, for this reason, quite unfitted for the passage of waggons, and was so not used by us. On the banks of the Umlatoosi, our camp lay in a hollow, commanded by hills and precipitous cliffs, and one where, had the Zulus attempted an attack, we should have had some trouble. Extra precautions had to be taken, all of which were luckily not needed, and on the following day we climbed slowly up the opposite hill, quite two miles long, and a fair earnest of what lay before us. The top reached after much struggling and cracking of whips, and the cool air blows in from the sea, not much more than fifty miles distant; while a fresh and quite unique panorama lies in front. Very broken indeed was the landscape; of flat ground there was absolutely none. The foreground was a long valley, its centre marked by a donga, deep and wide, in which a stream was visible. Towards this, winding excessively, ran lateral dongas, the intervening ground rising like swells at sea when there is no wind to break their tops. Thus the valley, which was some ten miles across, and twenty or more in length, was cut up checkerwise into irregular oblong patches, alike only in their unvaried sameness. The dongas on the left rose in Ibabanango, now behind—those meeting them from a detached ridge, along which our march was to lead. Uniting this with the hill-top on which we stood was a very narrow neck, some way below us, and already white with the tents of Wood's column. Over the whole, the dirty yellow-brown of a Zulu winter was spread. Far in the distance some mountain-ranges could be made out, clouds floating above them in the deep blue sky, the only thing of colour there.

On the highest point of the road stood a group of officers, field-glasses at work, looking out for something not easily seen as yet; and the often-repeated question went round and round with no answer—" Where is Ulundi? "It lay somewhere at the end of the valley below, but where, none could make out; indeed so well hidden was it by the hills round, that few saw it until the Umvolosi was crossed, just an hour or two before the battle.

On the narrow neck of land below was built the next post, Fort Evelyn, a neat little structure, principally put up by Wood's column, and so named after him. In times to come under our new commander, these names got to be much cavilled at, the new-comers asserting that it was somewhat impertinent to christen them after those who had been at the time principally interested in their construction; and we had Forts Victoria, George, Cambridge, and so on, by which to call the usual earthen erections near the camps, and which must have soon fallen down again when once the troops had left. Some amusement was caused by the terrible hurry to be in time which these new arrivals showed; the heliograph flashing its constant messages as what we were to do, and also not to do—all of which Lord Chelmsford appeared to treat in a delightfully polite manner, at which it must have been difficult to take offence. The amusement was not lessened when we heard of the desperate attempt to land at Port Durnford, and its failure— the picture of the "cocked-hats" for hours there in a small boat tossing freely being really ludicrous. The feeling prompting all this was natural enough. Under our then chief we had waited, worked, and fought; and it was hard on him as on us to see another come, hot-haste at the eleventh hour, to snatch our victory all ready prepared to hand.

At a distance, no doubt, our delays and caution did seem excessive; but to any one on the spot who could see the difficulties in the way of an advancing army through such a wonderful country as was Zululand where we crossed it, they would appear sheer necessities. Our way for twenty miles after leaving Fort Evelyn lay along the top of a narrow ridge, crossed by the most eccentric hills; one near the starting-point, known as "Jacko," as steep as any roof, and consuming a whole day to get up. The oxen were powerless, and had to be replaced by men, who toiled willingly enough at this tedious and irksome work.

On either side of our path the hills ran down to an ocean of broken ground, quite impassable, seamed with deep valleys, their bottom seldom to be seen, owing to their narrow, precipitous sides. Cliffs here and there cut into the mountain, and lessened our front to half its breadth just at the place where an attack might be expected. Water was scarce and bad; herbage short and insufficient; the night air terribly trying to our cattle: everything in nature was against us.

Just before reaching Entonjaneni, where the ridge ended and the descent to the Umvolosi commenced, was the track branching off south to St Pauls, and where it had been arranged that General Crealock with the 1st Division should meet our own. But the place was as solitary as the rest; no friendly column was, there, and the query for many days after was, "Where is Crealock?" It was this track that Scott-Douglas took when riding in the customary clouds from Fort Evelyn to camp, and on which, some twelve miles away, he met his sad, untimely death.

Landmarks there were none, even without the fog; the track was much defaced by the hoofs of the cattle out grazing; and the wonder is, that the accident did not happen more frequently. Thirteen miles from Entonjaneni was the Umvolosi, a broad sparkling river, its banks covered several miles deep with cactus and thorn trees, and a nasty place to get through with an army. Once safely on its banks, with a strongly-intrenched fort on our own side in case of reverse, and there was nothing left to do but to wade knee-deep across the water, and meet our till then invisible foe five miles farther on.

The story has been often told, and has lost nothing in the telling. Some, to suit their own tastes, have declared that it was nothing at all; a mass of well-trained soldiers against a naked mob of savages armed with knives. Numbers have been exaggerated unduly, or cut down into a mere handful. The slain have been counted by thousands, and also by hundreds. Every one tells the tale after his own wishes, whether right or wrong, but the truth remains that it was a "great victory," and with it went down for ever the Zulu race. Not a shot was fired after that day. The people returned to their homes quite contented; we were the "best men;" "we won't fight any more with such brave men; you have beaten us: let us be friends; and then go away."

In every post we had established in our rear, it was known that something was happening at the front. All day long on the memorable 4th July the air was full of rumours, and the men moved about more silently than usual, as if their attention was somewhere beyond their work. Every little cloud of dust on a hillside, raised by an approaching horseman, was eagerly watched; and as he came near, quiet groups would gather whereabouts he must pass, to catch any bits of news he might have.

"Look, Bill," I heard one group saying,—"look how he's riding,—and looking behind him! They aint far off after him, I know!"

It was known all down the line that the army was to cross the Umvolosi on that day, and the Zulu boast was that no white man ever lived to recross it. So a fight there must be.

Scouts on Ibabanango reported that a large *kraal* in the direction of Ulundi had been burning all day, and masses of natives had been seen in the same direction streaming over the hills. Then towards evening the heliograph flashed a message, "Ulundi in flames: Division was attacked on all sides; the enemy repulsed, with slight loss to ourselves." After that short sentence the sun went down, and we heard no more that night, knowing only that it was our chief and our army that had beaten the Zulus.

The morning of the 5th July broke tardily, and a thick fog shrouded everything up. The men pacing the line of parapet in the fort clapped their hands together, vainly trying to beat some little life into them, and stamped about, impatient for the bugle to sound "disperse." Through the mist the cooks' fires gleamed—the figures round them spectral and indistinct. Even the horses appeared to feel the dull, damp cold, and jerked uneasily at their head-ropes.

Things were at their dampest when some shapes grew out of the fog round the lunette which faces the front, and coming nearer, resolved themselves into a party of our Lancers —their faces streaming, their horses' coats dripping with moisture, and the little coloured pennons hanging down from the lance-heads without a ruffle.

And in the middle of the group rode a man, stout and thick-set, dressed in a grey mackintosh, his cap drawn over his face and ears, and his back bent double with fatigue. It was Forbes in from the battle, having ridden through the night some fifty miles, to be the first to bring the news of the battle of Ulundi. When he had dismounted and was taken into a tent, the officers put him down in the only easy-chair possessed, gave him tea and food, and gathered round to hear the story. Outside in the grey fog a group of men in greatcoats, and ammunition-pouches buckled to their waists, crept up to the tent-ropes, and crouching down listened, all ears, to the low words inside.

Just at first he was interrupted by such queries as, "Any one in the 94th?" "Who is the Major in the 58th?" "What about Wyatt-Edgell?" And a sigh of relief went round when it was known that he was the only one killed.

Once when a questioner went beyond the limits of a single question, the pent-up anxiety of the rest found utterance,—" Oh, don't interrupt; let him go on!"

"Not a sword but what was bloody when the 17th rode back," was heard, and taken approvingly as an avenging postscript to the Lancer's fall. With slow utterance—perhaps habit, perhaps the influence of fatigue—Forbes told the story in paragraphs, sipping his coffee and munching at the bread and marmalade just at the most thrilling points; so it seemed to the listeners.

We moved forward in "square" four deep; and as soon as it was evident the Zulus were going to attack, the odd numbers in the rear rank moved up alongside their front-rank men, the other two ranks standing where they were: thus the square had a side of three ranks—the front one elbow to elbow, the rear two with intervals. The two ranks next the enemy knelt down, and our square was complete. In the centre were the ammunition-carts, the cavalry, the Native Contingent, the two chaplains, and the stretchers, field-hospital, and attendant doctors.

The Zulus appeared on the hills round like bees, some three miles distant, advancing slowly in an echelon of companies, with a concave front towards us. After once in motion, the horns of this echelon moved gradually to the front of the main body, keeping together in compact order, and circling round the square till it was completely surrounded.

A reserve of two regiments of young men, armed with assegais only, made for the river, and were posted so as to cut off our line of retreat across it.

Everything was done without noise, hurry, or the slightest confusion. Here and there we could see a big fellow on a horse directing. Then the completed circle advanced with incredible swiftness, the men gliding through the long grass and taking advantage of every inequality of the ground. Nothing half so good is to be seen at Aldershot. Simply "skirmishing perfected." All at once the square opened fire, and the din commenced. The shriek of the slugs was easily distinguished from the "*ping*" of the

Martini rifles and the roar of the elephant guns. Overhead the lead flew past in clouds, fortunately for us. The Zulus, delivering this rain, crept up to within about eighty yards, almost unseen in the grass, just rising to fire and dropping instantly. At that distance they halted, and crept behind some low-bushes, out of which they pelted away pretty harmlessly, though much to their own loss, as our volleys directed into these bits of cover knocked them over in groups. Five minutes or a little more the brave fellows stuck to the place; then they wavered before our blazing, deadly wall of fire, and our soldiers seeing the movement through the intervals of smoke, set up an English cheer. That cheer, long and hearty, proclaimed the relief of nerves kept at their utmost stretch for the past three months. Then the square opened out and let forth the cavalry, which swept across the just occupied ground; and in fifty minutes from its commencement the battle was won.

A Zulu wearing a battered wideawake hat exposed himself to the fire of a whole face, receiving the bullets rained at him with derision, and eventually retreating unhurt.

A soldier of the 13th, in the middle of the firing coolly stepped to the front, knelt down, and took a deliberate aim at the Zulus, just as unconcerned as though it were the target he was practising at.

Another soldier being hit in the cheek by a bullet, turned to his officer and began to beg his pardon, thinking that the latter had hit him with his sword for inattention.

Two parsons standing in the centre of the square, by the side of their horses, were overheard in the din to say, "Oh, Mr Blank, isn't this awful?"

In one corner were the wounded lying on stretchers, the doctors about, with their sleeves tucked up, and their arms over blood—a ghastly sight.

The day before, when Buller was out, the Zulus had taunted our Basutos, crying out to them, "You curs! to-morrow we will drive you across the Blood river, and we will eat up all the red soldiers!"

After the fire ceased the next day, some 15,000 of them

were swarming up the hills away from the cavalry, only to meet with our shells, which naturally created no small panic as they pitched right among them—one Zulu telling me afterwards that twenty-seven men went down to one alone.

All this time the men were cheering and clapping loudly as each shell burst.

Nodwengo, a huge *kraal* with sides 1000 yards long, was blazing on one side of us; Ulundi, somewhat smaller, on the other; in front a third, "Panda's *kraal*," as it is called, was sparkling.

No prisoners were taken. Hours after the battle the popping of the Basutos' carbines told of the horrible kind of warfare we were engaged in. Merciless savages are these Basutos, though brave soldiers, and not a few of them Christians. But war to the death is their motto, one and all. One of them happened to hit a wretched Zulu in the legs as he was running away, and captured him. Sitting down beside his prize he pulled out some meat and a bit of biscuit and took his lunch, conversing all the while in a pleasant, friendly way with the Zulu, pumping him by asking all sorts of questions, and talking of old times when they might have met. Lunch over and the questions disposed of, the Basuto tightened his girths, put the bit into his pony's mouth, and nodding to his poor captive, said he must be off, as time pressed,—and without more ado took up his carbine and shot him dead.

Amongst those lying on the field after the battle were numbers of fine, handsome young men; the older men had all been for submission, and did not show up. The teeth of most were perfect, of the purest white, and regular —a chance missed by many an enterprising dentist.

"I should say there were 800 dead, as I saw them," was Forbes's estimate of the killed; and one not far out either way, I should say.

Then he said he must be going on, and the question was asked about horses, on which he half pulled out some papers from his breastpocket and said that he was the bearer of despatches from Lord Chelmsford to the Queen, the Prince of Wales, and a lot more big people, whereon he got his wish and his horse, and rode off towards Natal. He had not been gone ten minutes when the officer bearing the despatches rode in, the question on his lips, "Has that beggar Forbes been here, and taken my horse? Confound him, he did just the same at the last fort, and I can't catch him! "The artful Forbes was too many for the ordinary official mind, and was down before any one.

Next day the *Times* and the *Telegraph* tumbled in, followed by the *Illustrated News*; and so the battle had to be fought many times over and over again.

No sooner was the battle over than we dug a grave and buried our dead in the centre of the square, and then moved it bodily a little to the front, in a mild bravado, which could say afterwards that we licked the enemy and followed him up. Had we really done so in earnest, there is little doubt but that we should have caught Cetewayo, who had witnessed the fight from a distance; and, plucky to the last, on seeing himself defeated, told his body-guard to save themselves—he was too fat? to bolt, and would remain and give himself up. But Lord Chelmsford thought it wiser to be content: he had no food beyond the actual day, and Amanze Kanze, the new *kraal*, and said to be impregnable, was only fourteen miles ahead. So we trudged back through the dead bodies, and got to our *laager* on the right bank of the White Umvolosi.

This backward movement, when the war was not seemingly finished, had not the best effects on our spirits; all would have liked to have gone on and put an end to the whole affair. Our men were transformed into heroes: before Ulundi they looked behind them at the mention of a Zulu; now they thought only how they could get at him.

Amongst our allies, too, fear of the same people had been succeeded by an indifference almost ludicrous. Before Ulundi, when you called out, "Zulu, Johnnie!" to a native picket, the men shook their heads, as if it was no joking matter; after it was over they would show their teeth, and shout back a regular "view-halloo"—"Ah, ah, Johnnie ! Zulu gone away."

Still scraps of the old feeling showed out now and then: an

old Scotchman on sentry reported, I remember, that he could see Zulu fires on the hill in front of his post, and when asked if he could hear anything, said, "Indeed I did, sir,— I heard a sort of quiet clashing of swords in the donga."

The pluckiest of our allies were the Basutos; and they were delighted with the battle. They sat on their tiny ponies inside the square when the firing went on, dodging from side to side to watch the effect of the shots, just like figures hung on wires. "Now," they said, "red soldier fight proper; beforetime he send out Basuto to go fight for him, and be killed, while he stay in *laager*; now he make *man-laager* himself, and he put Basuto inside, and tell him, 'You eat biscuit, and we fight d—d Zulu.'"

The confidence with which we were attacked was amusing: a little more, and it might have been terrible. There is no doubt that we selected the identical spot for the battle which Cetewayo had himself previously chosen; and the omen was thought, by his men, to be particularly favourable. The men moved with the utmost deliberation till our square was surrounded. Mules and ponies, ready saddled, were provided for the pursuit; the women begged to be allowed to stop, as they had heard so much of the red soldiers, and wanted to see them: everything pointed to an expected easy victory. But our *laager* was too strong for them; it was sheltered by a steel shield, off which they saw their bullets drop like rain-drops: we had stopped up all the previous night loading our rifles, and so shot too fast. One man told me, "I was coming on, when pop came a bullet over my shoulder, and my brother, on the right of me, dropped dead; then pop came another, over my left shoulder, and the man there dropped too; so I ran away: then came a 'by-and-by,' and killed twenty-three of us; so we all ran away further still."

At Entonjaneni—that bleakest of bleak plateaus—we were caught in a three days' storm of rain and clouds. The cold was intense, the tents saturated, our clothes wet through and through, and the oxen died by hundreds.

Chapter Fourteen
Battlefield

Wood with his column struck off south to Kwamagwasa and St Pauls by the road on which General Crealock was so long expected, while General Newdigate took his division back by the road it came, and sat down once more on the banks of the Upoko.

Everything was in a state of disintegration. Chaos and uncertainty reigned supreme; and I think one and all wished that our chief, under whom we had fought at Ulundi, were still with us, instead of the new man sent out to replace him. Our tarnished, wayworn gold-lace and clothes looked dreadfully dull beside the brand-new uniforms of his staff, but just landed from a comfortable ship, with many boxes, and new kits.

Life, too, became utterly wearisome from its monotony. Every day is as like the preceding one as two peas. At 5.15 A.M. comes reveille— that most dismal of bugle-sounds—and every one springs up ready dressed, and struggles out of his tent, through an opening tightened by the night dew, and wet in proportion. Probably a fog is hanging about, and a cold wind blowing; and if there is no moon, it will be very dark. The men "fall in by sections" to have the roll called, and then move off silently into their places, fixing bayonets as they come up. At the door of every tent stands the "poleman," his duty to pull away the pole and run into cover with it on an alarm. The cavalry have stood to their horses, saddling up, ready for a start: the gunners stand round their guns. Not a word is spoken. Outside the *laager* the cooking-fires are being lighted, and their glow is a pleasant contrast to the prevailing gloom.

Then the General, with some of his staff, walks round, and the men resign themselves to a weary wait. The officers, in groups, shrug their shoulders inside their greatcoats, and wonder, for the fiftieth time, how long this thing is going to last. Then, after much waiting, the dawn shows in the east, and with it springs up a cold frosty air that nips one's finger-ends and makes one's ears tingle. Coffee passes the time till the hills grow out distinct enough to show any advancing foe; and that settled, the men are let off, and disappear inside their tents. Sweepers turn out and broom away vigorously; the ration-bugle sounds, and "orderly-men" double off to draw the daily beef and bread. Trumpets sound the "feed" to the neigh of the horses, who know the call as well as their betters. Then the sun tops the last hill-crest, and sets to work to warm us all up.

There are the mails to despatch, carried by tiny ponies, led by others ridden by almost naked Kafirs, their great toes in the stirrups—if extra swells, with one spur on a naked heel. Vedettes have to be posted; the report of the incoming mounted men to be listened to; the night pickets to be withdrawn; the natives perched a mile away in some snug cranny to be sent for. A troop of Lancers is told off to a convoy of waggons, and files steadily past towards the river to get a drink before starting. On the hillside, outside the camp, the "boys" are busy inspanning their mules. Behind them is riding, as fast as a tired horse will allow, some one bound homewards or to the front; cavalry men riding hard with despatches. And in the midst of all this Pat Murphy salutes you with the news that "breakfast is served."

The meal over—only cold stewed beef from yesterday's dinner, coffee with tinned milk if you have any, and the luxury of a pot of jam —and the day begins.

The travellers depart; the working-parties set out; a lot of waggons have to be "offloaded" or "loaded up;" boards of officers assemble to ascertain damages; the "defaulters" file past, carrying sacks in which to gather the rubbish littering the camp and deposit it in pits ready dug by others; cavalry are hard at work cleaning out their lines: cleanliness in our stationary camps, crowded with dirt-producing creatures, came before godliness. The herd of slaughter-oxen are dodging the butcher in a hollow, who, rifle in hand, watches long for a shot. Reports from the signallers on the hill drop in. A spy is brought up, and causes some small excitement among the men, glad to relieve the intense monotony. Then comes dinner, a mere repetition of breakfast. Work again till four, when the men once more "man the *laager,*" teas—only boiling water and biscuit; a chat till "tattoo" at eight, when every one tumbles between as many blankets as he has been able to "beg, borrow, or steal," and gets what sleep he can in his tight boots and not over-pleasant tunic.

Some days—red-letter days, far between—the English mail came in, and we hurried with treasures into quiet corners to get away from Zululand for five minutes. Or again, a party will start on their ponies, with carbines slung over their shoulders, in hopes of a chance shot at a buck or a *paauw*; sometimes a foraging excursion with the Lancers after reported cattle hidden away in a valley. One solace was denied us; there was no liquor in the camp to speak of, and so the social glass at night was not to be had—and talking without anything but cold tea or weak coffee is apt to come to an end pretty shortly.

Apropos of teetotal principles, a capital article appeared about that time in a weekly paper, called "Wooden War;" its drift that our generals are too prone to follow a rigid system, applicable everywhere when on the war-path; so to say, taking Aldershot about in their pockets. The paper had special reference to the mistakes in Zululand, and ended by saying that "nowhere can it be impossible to dig ditches of sufficient width to frustrate an active enemy, or to place obstacles which will hinder his advance. Grass may be twisted into ropes, bushes pinned down, pits dug, stakes planted, and broken bottles strewn."

Now the peculiarities of Zululand do not admit of one of these expedients. The ground is so hard and solid, that to dig a small pit is a day's labour; grass grows thinly, and is the reverse of an obstacle to a Zulu even when twisted—an arrangement indeed they used more than once against ourselves; to find a piece of wood fit to make a stake would be a week's journey— and the stake, if found, would inevitably be "jumped" on the first night; while empty bottles did not exist, simply because there were no full ones. Thus much to show how strange a country our generals had to make war in. We ragged ones used to look with envy on the pictures in the *Illustrated News* about the Afghan war. There the mess-tent of some regiment was shown, wherein was an officer digging into a plump ham; several servants handing round "Simpkin;" and most striking of all, a tablecloth on the table. Why, there was not a mess in Zululand, unless it were the General's; our waiters were "Tommy Atkins," simple and fairly pure; a ham would have commanded the price of a dinner for six at the Club if it had put in an appearance; and as for liquor, well—it was spoken of under one's breath that Wood drank champagne every night, only we did not believe it. Lucky the man who had a little bad rum; he will have many friends, and will not go, as we did go so often, wet, cold, and cheerless to bed.

The craving for jam was insatiable, and rather expensive. The few tins which remained after Ulundi were beyond price. It must be remembered that we had entered the land more than a month ago with an allowance of twenty pounds apiece for stores and cooking-pots, and the latter weigh heavily. Men at home who "never touch sweets," in Zululand treasured up a pot of jam as a miser does gold.

"Jam!" cried a well-known correspondent, "I have not tasted it for weeks; don't bring it out, or I shall finish the pot!" It came of the want of vegetable food. Beef, nothing but beef. We catch our ox one day, kill and eat him on the next, and repeat the operation on every succeeding day.

As we were out foraging on the way up, we came to a *kraal* in which were two old Zulu women, left behind to die, as was often the case amongst men who have no reverence for age. A young man will come into the *kraal*, and seeing his old mother cowering over the fire, will coolly take her by the neck and pitch her outside, so that he may in turn squat in her place. One of the men, seeing a stone which evidently covered a hole with grain stowed away inside, pulled it away, and inserting his arms hauled out with a great pull—not a bundle of mealies, but—a baby's head. The poor little thing had been hastily buried in the hole used in peace-time for storing grain.

The *kraal* itself was some fifteen miles east of Isandlwana, and from the neck of land above a capital view was to be seen down the valley in which Lord Chelmsford was on that unhappy day.

The valley ran up to a point almost under where we stood—its sides so steep that the bottom was quite hidden. On the opposite side it towered into a great flat-topped mountain, fearfully stony, and utterly barren. On a shelf in the cliff below was a large *kraal*, with a path to it, which ran up what looked to be a sheer precipice. Over the huts the big mountain hung, impassable and repulsive. Great boulders, painted red by nature, lay about its sides, piled up, or lying close together like paving-stones. Galleries, scarped in the same naked rock, ran round the edge of the mountain-top. Avalanches or fragments poured down the scores made in its face by everlasting storms. Not a bush or a blade of grass hid up its naked horrors.

The valley below soon opened out into broad space: entirely yellow, carpeted with the eternal dry grass; netted with *dongas* cut and scrawled in the red earth; here and there a *kraal* in the middle of mealie-fields. Two thorn-trees stood out alone to relieve the monotony. Down the middle ran a small river, its water sparkling with life and freedom. Further away the valley was brought to an abrupt end by a range of mountains, rising in masses, bare, and seemingly precipitous. A fringe of forest-trees ran along their crest, showing that the southern slopes were wooded. These are the hills which look down on the Tugela, and across the plain on which Etshowe nestles, full fifty miles away.

But in all that wonderful panorama there was not a sign of life. The beaten ground about the *kraals* was empty; the fields were without labourers, the pasturage without cattle. Even the very dogs were gone with their absent masters.

Following the valley-line on our side, we found the granite built into a wall fifty feet high, with blocks as neatly squared as if by hand—the hands of giants. In every crevice were flame-coloured flowers, erect, and tinting the grey stone with a pale reflection of their own glories. A troop of a dozen buck bounded out of a grassy shelf, throwing back their heads and whisking their short white tails. Below was the valley we had come by, lit up with the fire of burning *kraals* or the blazing grass, across which the flames licked like a great wave. The Lancers, off-saddled nearer at hand in a mealie-field, looked like coloured dots. Beyond, again, Ibabanango rose and hid any further view. The hills were dotted with yellow "everlastings," and the moist crannies by the stream nourished clusters of maidenhair ferns. A brace of wild duck floated in a pool hard by, and some half-dozen *paauw* rose from a recently-burnt patch and flapped away. Quail started everywhere under foot; and a species of plover, with black-and-white plumage, was temptingly tame. On another hill was an ant-bear taking his evening stroll. He was a curious creature, as large as a good-sized dog, with a round back, long snout, and thick bushy hair and tail. When we rode for him, he made off at a good pace—skipping and rolling, and flinging his nose in the air most comically. In the end he turned sharp into his hole, and we could hear him digging furiously, and grunting, as if terribly put out at being hustled so rudely.

As we left the country, now divested of its own inhabitants, the game began to return. On our way to Ulundi we seldom saw any; now buck and *paauw* were quite plentiful. Wild turkeys —as they call a kind of black curlew—were not uncommon: they have a blood-red knob on their heads as large as a pigeon's egg, which probably gives them their name, and are, moreover, capital eating. In the rocks live little "rock-rabbits"—strange, grey-coated creatures, without tails, and sharp teeth—pro- ? bably the conies mentioned in the Bible. Besides these were a few hares, reddish-brown, and very tiny; here and there a troop of hartebeests, and monkeys in the cliffs: so the country is not altogether desolate.

Westward, across a steep range of hills, broken into many valleys and stone-faced terraces, lies the plain about Isandlwana— the rock itself rising some ten miles away. The range we crossed ends to the north in the grand Isipezi—its precipices and crag-terraces hard and distinct in the clear atmosphere. In front is the wide valley, sloping down gently towards the Buffalo, running unseen between steep banks. The farther side of this great plain rises to meet a low, broken ridge, which grows bolder and more mountainous towards Isandlwana, and was the cover behind which the Zulus came on that day. The whole valley, some seven miles in breadth, was carpeted with yellow grass, waving slowly to and fro as the wind stole across. Here and there a reef of rocks cropped up; a donga, sharply cut out of the prevailing tint, straggled down the centre in an endless maze of twists and turns. To all appearance, the floor of the valley is entirely level; yet on closer acquaintance you find it is made up of folds of ground large enough to conceal an army—the level bits are singularly few. Dingy patches are the mealie-fields, in which the ripe grain was still uncut: the whole place far and near appeared accursed. Even the Zulus have forsaken it; and the few ant-hills which from their size alone you know to be *kraals*, seem to have been long deserted. In the whole landscape there was no sign of life.

Towards the Buffalo the valley widens, though it still retains its uniform slope and tint, which, from utter sameness, is wearisome, and the eye rests for relief on the plateau beyond, which is Natal.

In the same direction is Isandlwana, seemingly detached from the rest by some freak of nature. Black and solitary, it stands alone. Its shape, like the roof of a pent-house or lean-to, is lit up with the morning sun on this the Zulu side, and every crack and cranny is distinct.

The tramp to it through the long grass—over beds of loose stones, ant-bear holes, and *dongas*—was tedious; and the everlasting folds of ground which rose one after the other in front, tiring to a degree. But still, whatever were the accidents of ground we met, there was that strange landmark ever before us.

On nearing the rock, you cross a river over a drift cut in its banks for the passage of waggons. A little farther a second stream is passed, its bed made practicable with stones. *Dongas* across the path have been levelled, and a track made over them. The road is no longer on the pathless veldt, but is distinctly marked. It was, in fact, laid out, and the drifts cut, by the army which lay there in January, and was to have led it onward into Zululand.

From the point where the road is met, it leads straight for the hill: on the right, full half a mile away, is an artillery-cart, hauled thus far by the Zulus, and then abandoned in the long grass. A gun-limber, marked N. 5, R.A.—the number of the 7-pounder battery we lost—stood in the middle of the road, at least a mile from the camp : one limber-box is still in its place, the other, broken open, lies a hundred yards farther on. Near this limber, in a tuft of grass just off the road, lay, full length, the body of a Zulu warrior. It was little but a skeleton; but the skin still stretched tightly across the frame and face, while a plume of black ostrich-feathers adhered to the scalp.

After this one the bodies lay more thickly,— all in patches of rank grass six feet high. Where the men fell in groups, the grass is very thick. The Carabineers, who fell fighting bravely in a circle, with Durnford in the midst, lay a little apart. Wherever an ox or a horse had been killed, there was a patch; and the whole field was covered with these tell-tale patches.

Leaving the gun-carriage behind, the road comes on a *kraal* and its mealie-garden. The *kraal* was destroyed, but the Kafir corn in the field round it was ripe and nodding. Close in front was the slope which lies under the rock, and the neck of land, a couple of hundred yards in length, connecting it with the conical hill which looks down on Fugitives' Drift. Both were studded with waggons, scattered about in the utmost confusion, —some empty, many loaded up—amongst the latter several containing grain; the bags had rotted, and the oats falling out, had filled the waggons with black mould, from which the green leaves were springing brightly. In many waggons the oxen had been assegaied in the yokes, and lay in two ghastly rows, eight of a side, just as they fell. The skins were perfect, while through the assegai-holes could be seen their last meal, now turned into chopped hay,—for all the world looking as if they had been stuffed.

Horses lay like the oxen, stabbed at their picket-lines; some knee-haltered,—killed as they hobbled away, their necks still tied to their foreleg. By the side of some lay the black grooms, mere skeletons,—the bit of red rag round their skulls showing which side they were on. The soldiers had nearly all been buried by their own regiment, which asked to pay this last act of respect to its own dead. The ground was too hard to dig graves in it: the bodies were laid in a donga, and the sides thrown in to cover them. What bodies there were had their clothes on, stripped only, in cases, of the red coats. The horrid picture that appeared, in which the bodies were shown lying almost naked, with an assegai sticking out of each, is an utter fabrication.

On one side was the line of cooking-places,—the ashes lying in heaps, the firewood piled alongside. In the centre of the camp were mealie-fields and *kraals*, since destroyed. On the left, as you faced the hill, were the round places on which stood the officers' tents. These had been cut off all round the bottom, and the top removed; but the circle remained strewed with cheque-books, army-lists, ledgers, and heaps of papers. In one stood a camp-bed, in another White's campaigning-bag; boots lay everywhere; brushes were very plentiful; camp-chairs, a pair of crieketing-pads, a Prayer-book, lay about, mixed up with ammunition-boxes and ox-hide shields. These ammunition-boxes lay everywhere, far and near, all empty,—the tin-case ripped open, as if the Zulus, in their eagerness for the contents, had rushed off out of the melee, and hastily broken them open. Opposite the officers' tents were the men's, cut down, as were the former,—littered with bayonet-scabbards, thick boots, pocket-ledgers, pipeclay boxes, and all the small trifles which a soldier possesses.

The band-tent was strewn with music; and on one side lay the half of a large brass instrument, sadly battered. The hospital was easily distinguished,—each medicine-chest, with its red cross, being tossed about, burst open, and the contents scattered round.

All amongst this debris were waggons, dead drivers, oxen, horses, and heaps of litter blown by the wind; and most unmistakable of all, the clumps of tall grass, bright yellow, each hiding its own dead. Grain in patches was springing near the horse-lines, green and beautiful; beyond, the waving sea of yellow,—never still—always the same.

The position chosen for the camp is worth noting, as it has been foolishly spoken against as one of the primary causes which led to our defeat there.

Standing among the debris of the tents, facing Zululand, and with our backs against the rock, we see on the left, about a mile distant, the range of hills on which the Zulus deployed for the attack when first seen. A ridge, steep towards the rear, connects this range with the rock; itself some 400 yards long, and perhaps half as much in height, if so much—only to be climbed with difficulty at one point. Behind us on the right is the neck which connects the rock with a round hill on the extreme right of the camp, and close to it. This neck is only 100 yards across, and looks down on the road which leads to Rorke's Drift; the ascent to it is perfectly bare, open, and very steep. In front the ground slopes away into Zululand in a gradual slope, quite open and unprovided with cover. It was fifteen miles in this direction, among the hills which enclose the valley, that Lord Chelmsford and the greater part of the army spent the day.

On the extreme right, the Buffalo, running between banks almost perpendicular, closed the way.

Thus, had the troops held the neck with a slight force supported by an intrenchment, an enemy would have found the front of the camp alone open to an attack—their advance, moreover, having to climb a sloping glacis, perfectly open on all sides, and specially adapted to artillery or musketry fire. No better position need have been wished for had only precautions been taken against an attack from the rear; indeed those left behind by Lord Chelmsford were in rare spirits at seeing the Zulus coming on, thinking it the height of good-luck to be in for such a "good thing" while more than half of them were away. And it was only when the "right horn" of the attack showed over the neck and took them in flank and rear that the English felt otherwise. Five minutes after this terrible "horn" came up and the cries had ceased, there was not a white man alive at Isandlwana.

Chapter Fifteen
To the Connaughts

Now no sooner had Ulundi been fought than every one who was able to get away did so. It was quite evident that the Zulu war was over. The new arrivals with Sir Garnet were somewhere down country hoping for a fight, could one be got up; but it could not be done. The Zulus to a man said they had had enough; we were the "best men;" we had licked them fairly, so now we might go away. And go away we did. Forbes led the way; the rest of the correspondents followed fast. The flying column was broken up; and the 13th, after three years "on the *veldt*," was off home. Wood and Buller, clever fellows, followed. Lord Chelmsford and his staff were bound seaward. Stores, piled high in the roadside forts, were loaded and sent back whence they came. Our old friends the Native Contingent—Searle's Anabomvas, the Swazies with their feather-plumes, and Shepstone's Basutos, invaluable as scouts—pass down to be disbanded; and we did not lose these old friends without some feeling of sadness. Weary nights had we spent on picket alongside one another; miles had we trudged round their sentries behind an *Induna*, who, with a blanket only as his uniform, brushed over the stones and wringing grass. Morning after morning, when we were shivering in the shelter-trench round the *laager*, have we watched the curious procession of their companies, each headed by a man with a small calico flag—each native rolled up into a shapeless bundle, his legs sticking out of one end, his sheaf of assegais out of the other. Time after time had we watched the nimble Basutos canter out at early dawn, to scour the country, and light our way by the blaze of burning *kraals*. We knew all their watchwords— "Koss," "Queen," "Number nine"—and had called out in fun to them a hundred times, "Halloa, Johnnie!" They were all Johnnie to the soldiers, and the soldiers all Johnnies to them. Even the

Zulus had picked up the term, and called out as they came on at Kambula, "Don't run away, Johnnie; we want to speak to you." Buller's followers, too, went fast, and we missed their rough and ready faces; their velveteen uniforms, belted with the invariable bandoleer of cartridges; and their shaggy little ponies, seemingly never used up, always ready for a gallop.

Then we got up a race-meeting at the Upoko, where was General Newdigate and his rapidly melting division — the card including "The Assegai Stakes," "The Intombie or Maiden Cup," "The Slow Barney Handicap," and "The Ketchwayo Consolation Welter." Twenty-five Basutos, I remember, started for one race, and tumbled off nearly to a man at the first fence.

Never did a body of men feel more inclined to join in the cry, "The king is dead!—long live the king!" than did we. A month or more previously we had set our faces towards home after Ulundi. The Zulu army had been defeated, its organisation broken, Cetewayo a fugitive. Nothing more for the victors but to march away to civilisation, to be feted on their success. When lo! up starts a fresh general, and inaugurates a fresh campaign. There would be fighting yet. Cetewayo had bolted, but might reorganise a fresh army. His last stronghold, Amanze Kanze, remained untaken. His best lieutenant, Dable Amanze, had swaggered into the coast column more like a conqueror than a beaten nigger chief, and had demanded clothes. They gave him an ulster, and he demanded drink. They gave him a glass of "square-face," which he drank, and asked for more. They said it was a teetotal camp, and could give no more; on which the chief in his ulster threw down seven sovereigns, part of his Isandlwana gains, and told them that would pay for it. A few antiquated German guns, some blunderbusses, and half-a-dozen old sporting-guns, either burst or broken, had been given up, and nothing else. So the war must begin again.

Things being thus rather at a stand-still, I took the opportunity to ride to Etshowe through the country not yet visited lying between Kwamagwasa and the Umlatoosi, across which it was hoped a road existed. It was a long ride, nearly 160 miles there and back, and but scant accommodation on the way, but the

141

outfit was not extensive.

A blanket was folded under the saddle, another with the greatcoat rolled up, was strapped on behind. A feed of corn was hitched on one side; three squares of soup, a box of sardines, a flask of rum, and a toothbrush on the other: and this must last nine days. Board and lodging, on the ground, could be counted on at our posts: were there none, I had the *veldt*, good honest grass, with a few bushes for a fire, and, it was to be hoped, a fine sky.

The first part of my road was that traversed by the army in its advance to Ulundi. What grass there had been left by our cattle was burnt by the acre. Dead oxen lay about in ghastly attitudes, some preserved by the air just as they had fallen, others a heap of half-picked bones. Hungry dogs slunk away into the nearest *donga*, and vultures were perching on the rocks over the site of the camping-grounds.

The track was worn and polished across the grass by the traffic; wheel-tracks were everywhere, crossing and recrossing, straggling apart over the level bits, and drawing close together at the hills and defiles.

Every few miles came a patch, blacker and more untidy than the surrounding hills, marking the camps we occupied going or coming back. The shelter-trench was still round them, the corners marked by the epaulments thrown up by the artillery. Scattered about were glittering things, shining with dazzling brightness, for many a mile. They were the tin biscuit-cases, long since emptied, and left behind. My first night was spent at Fort Evelyn, our last post towards the front. The thing most striking about the Fort to a stranger was its ditch, which had come upon so many huge boulders in its course round the parapet as to be but a ditch by courtesy.

A large dog and a small mouse spent the night with me. The former was a monster with two expressionless wall-eyes and a benevolent face. The first time he came in, his nose got between my legs as I was turning in, and nearly capsized me. The second attempt landed him on my rugs in comfortable slumber. The third found him creeping through a place in the tent where the peg was wanting. The rest of the night he devoted to attempts at forcing an entrance at various points. In the intervals the mouse visited every part of the interior, and showed its satisfaction generally by a most indefatigable scratching.

Starting with the post next morning, a party of half-a-dozen irregulars leading ponies with the bags—for the road beyond the fort was not safe for single travellers—I bade adieu to my night's companions, and climbed the long ridge which leads to Entonjaneni. Clouds hung about the mountains, and hid out much that was ugly. Every here and there we passed the black and dismal camp-grounds. What view there was, was monotonous and depressing. There was no life, save a few lung-sick oxen left behind to die, and the sneaking curs. No trees, no bushes, no water. Nothing but dead grass, worn and polished by ten thousand feet.

Half-way we met a party from the post ahead, and having transferred the bags, rode on again, turning off the beaten track before long, and following a ridge which led due south to Kwamagwasa.

After riding along this new track for some time, the fog lifted, and a fresh country layabout. The hills are more rounded, the valleys deeper and narrower, the soil less arid, black and peaty where the streams cut through it, while *dongas* were almost entirely wanting.

Patches of bright indian-red clothed the hillsides; grass was springing fresh and green beside the red; the old familiar brown had vanished, to be replaced by a sheet of colour spread everywhere. Sunshine alone was wanting; colours in a fog are apt to become a little washy.

My escort were four Volunteer Horse, rough-looking men at first sight, in cord suits of a warm brown faced with scarlet, mounted on little ponies that somehow or other managed to scramble along at a fine pace. On closer acquaintance the troopers proved to be gentlemen, unshaved, not unlikely unwashed too; was I not all but the same? There was an ex-captain of the line, a young draughtsman from an engineer's office, and a couple of medical students from Trinity College. All had come out for

143

the fun of the thing; some had been promised commissions, others nothing; all had in the end to be content with berths in the Volunteer Horse, to be dressed in brown cords, and to carry the mails.

In the gullies small clumps of vegetation showed up as we went along—wild plantains, tree-ferns, and broad-leaved bushes, on which the eye dwelt with delight after the treeless waste we had left. On the sky-line in front, some dark forest-trees were prominent objects in the view, and marked the place where Kwamagwasa stood.

Before the war, Kwamagwasa was a mission-station; and as the trees round it grew more distinct, and the fog was left behind to cling to the bleak uplands of Entonjaneni, it soon became apparent that the missionaries had hit upon a chosen spot.

Round about, the land, smoothed of all creases, rolled itself into endless hills and valleys; nowhere was there a level bit. The road coiled endlessly along the crest of a ridge, rising and descending again for ever. Streams began to show in the hollows, betrayed as often by the bright foliage which hid them as by the sparkle of their water. Tree-ferns grew more luxuriantly, leading on to the dark trees in front, with which the line of a new watershed was fringed.

In the foreground were the blue-gum trees sheltering the mission-houses and church; to the left of these were the tents of the troops stationed there, dotting the slope of a conical hill; between the two points were two spurs, well wooded, containing a valley which ran away for miles, ever growing broader, to the distant hills. On a hill close by, the signallers were flashing messages to Fort Evelyn, the answering flash looking like Venus tethered to a hill-top. A small enclosure had been made on the top of an adjacent hill, and was known as Fort Robertson, after the missionary who lived opposite. Now his church was pulled down, his house was in ruins, and he himself lived in a waggon near Etshowe.

These ruins stand in the middle of a garden full of handsome shrubs; walks, shaded by blue-gums, lead to outlying houses perched romantically wherever a view was to be seen; fruit-trees grew luxuriantly; a patent plough lay in the corner of what was once the stable.

The buildings were of brick, those used in the church being better finished than the rest. At the end of the schoolhouse was a tablet, still in its place, telling that it was built in 1874 by Bishop Wilkinson. In the centre of the garden hung the church-bell, untouched by the Zulus, though hardly so much respected by our own men, who carried it off, and were not a little surprised when they were made to restore it. Sheets of corrugated iron strewed the ground. A patch, on which grew a crop of Cape gooseberries, was in one corner, and were found to make most excellent jam. Everywhere were charming peeps of hill and valley. Forest-trees grew everywhere near about. *Kraals* were plentiful: in many, Zulus had ventured to live once more, as the smoke curling upwards told. Herds of Zulu cattle, an unwonted sight, dotted the hills. Everything told of returning peace.

Birds fluttered among the trees, twittering as much of a song as a Zulu bird is capable of.

Flocks of scarlet-billed Avadavats flew about, dressed in the speckled brown coats which have given them the name of nutmeg-birds; thrushes, and Indian bulbuls with the bunch of yellow feathers under their tails; a sun-bird, like a gay humming-bird, gorgeous in green and golden ruffles. Spotted shrikes were plentiful, and quaker-coated doves cooed incessantly in the undergrowth.

Noticeable among the shrubs was the poin-settia, with its scarlet leaves; weeping-willows, then leafless; and above all, a tree whose leaves and branches were plated with frosted silver. The foliage grew like plumes, two feet or more high, shaped like the feathers in our hussars' busbies. It was of the pine species, and its cones, of a bright silver-grey, clung to the sides of the plumes. Some, riper than others, had opened, and between each of the scales was a puff of eider-down. The beauty of the tree proved its destruction, as the soldiers each carried away a bit in token of remembrance.

A sadder reminiscence are two rough wooden crosses which

mark the graves of Lieutenant Scott-Douglas and Corporal W. Cotter, the last a trooper of the 17th Lancers. Scott-Douglas, who was little more than a boy, was employed in signalling, and losing his way in the fog, on his way to the column, wandered thus far with his orderly. Ulundi had not then been fought, and the pair were caught by the Zulus and assegaied close to the spot where they now lie buried. Their graves are on a spur of the hill which stands out from the ridge on which Fort Robertson was built; around them are vast uplands waving high with grass; above are two trees, quaintly-shaped aloes, the only trees in that direction for many miles. Not a sound disturbs their rest; no foot is likely to come that way; silent and sad are the crosses over the soldier lad and his dead comrade. His death was one of our most sad episodes, and he was mourned by many.

All round Kwamagwasa the Zulus had come back in considerable numbers, bringing with them their women and cattle; indeed it was doubtful if many had not remained the whole time.

The method we adopted with them was to let them know that if they came into the fort and gave up their arms, passes guaranteeing their safety would be issued to them, and they would be allowed to go back to their *kraals*, which were to be subject to visits now and again to ascertain how they were conducting themselves, and that no more than the stipulated number allowed to return were living in the *kraal*; and with this system they appeared to be quite contented.

Their independence was capital, and almost laughable. Not one would sell us anything except at most exorbitant prices. They said out, without the smallest hesitation, "What more do you English want? You have beaten us fairly—we own that you are better at fighting than we are—so now go away!" As to compensation sought for by us, we might as well have asked for the moon. Like boys at a public school, they had had a fight to see who was the "best man:" that decided, nothing was left but to be the greatest friends, and be off. A Zulu offered to sell me an old cock, fearfully scraggy, in exchange for a pickaxe; while another refused a shilling for a bracelet made of a few common shells.

The regular road from Kwamagwasa to Natal bends due east, in order to descend the mountainous plateau to the valley of the Umlatoosi at St Paul's, the only point practicable for waggons. From that station it descends, crosses the river, and winds west again to Etshowe, some forty miles distant.

The trees round this latter place were plainly visible from Kwamagwasa, in a direct line due south; and it was this line which I had to follow. So, with an escort of half-a-dozen of my former Irregular friends, I bade farewell to the pretty Mission and its most hospitable garrison, and rode off, trusting to return on the third day.

At first we rode to a *kraal* a few miles on our way to obtain a guide, which, after some difficulty, we succeeded in. Then the head-man of the village was told to prepare with a friend to return to the fort, and to remain there as hostages for our safety. Anything happening to us was to be visited on the pair. That business settled after a tremendous wrangle, in which every old woman of the *kraal* took an animated part, we wished good-bye to those going back, and turning our own ponies' heads down a small precipice, over which our guide led at a trot, made for a distant mountain-range.

In front of our party trotted the Zulu guide, a fine strapping fellow, wearing an under-vest, probably taken at Isandlwana, and a black-and-white "*moucha*." On either side of him rode a trooper with his carbine unslung. The sun shone brightly; the grass was soft and green under our ponies' feet; the streams ran away with a tinkle, reminding us of home: all gave promise of a pleasant day.

Very broken was the country,—endless hill, endless dale, all grass-clad: cruel hills, which we had to climb; delightfully picturesque dingles, holding tree-ferns in profusion, which we went down into. On many of the spurs *kraals* were perched, surrounded by herds of black-and-white cattle, goats, and a few sheep. In all were Zulus. Some seemed content to watch us from a distance, others started at a run to catch us up.

One stalwart fellow came up after a run of good two miles

as little out of breath as if he had only stepped across the road. On asking him what he wanted, he replied—

"Only to look at you. When my king comes this way, I run out to look at him, or he kills me: so I come out to look at you." And look he did, every tooth in his jaws shining like ivory.

The people we met had a more pleasing expression, with far less of the cruel cunning in their faces, than those farther north. All were fat and flourishing. The horrors of war evidently had not penetrated to this out-of-the-way place.

All wore the "*moucha*" only—a kilt before and behind, made of black-and-white goatskin— and carried a snuffbox in a hole drilled through the lobe of one ear. Most of those who came to stare were lads of twenty or thereabouts; the married men, known by the ring round the head, were much more dignified, and squatted in groups round the *kraals*. At these were always black, merry urchins, staring timidly from a distance, and gaunt Kafir dogs, who looked upon us as enemies, and followed us barking and snarling most furiously.

I can liken the broken character of the country to nothing better than a stiff sheet of brown paper which has been rolled into a ball and then spread out again. The sheet thus treated would be a reproduction in miniature of the general features about us, except that the creases should run, not any way at all, but in a certain order.

The principal spurs sprang from the main ridge behind us, always sloping downwards and towards the same direction. From these spread other spurs, smaller and at right angles; while these, again, had their own little spurs standing out in exactly the same manner. Down one of these secondary spurs our path lay—always descending towards an elevated valley which lay across the foot of this jumble of hill and dale, itself topped again on the farther side by a range of mountains. The Zulu name for this range is Langwe, and from its crest you look down on the valley of the Umlatoosi, over which we had to go.

The track, invisible to us, wound over endless knolls, and across valleys with concave sides, very steep. *Kraals* were perched on elevated points; herds of cattle fed in the bottoms. The valleys towards the west held good-sized streams; patches of emerald on their banks told of water-meadows and rich pasture. Above these oases the mountains were rugged, and their sides seamed with watercourses. Black spots beyond, again, are forest-trees— an earnest of more to come. Everywhere else the grass threw its smooth colour over all. The mountain-top was decked out with flowers, amongst them bosses of heather with scarlet bells, double the size of our home varieties.

Another valley, across which we wind over a neck left obligingly for wayfarers, and we climb a second ridge. Far in front, on the very crest, we see a nick in the hill-top, evidently our road; and for this point the natives of the country appeared to be making also. Everywhere we saw bands of them hurrying along the ridges which led to the nick. Even in rear were more coming on in Indian file, at a run, as if afraid they might be late. I counted fifty at one time thus converging.

Our own road led along the slope of a spur which ever edged upwards: on one side a nasty fall, a lot of bush and high grass above. None of the visitors had arms, as far as we could see; so there was little cause for alarm. The men quietly unslung their carbines, while I undid the flap of my pistol, in case of necessity.

At length we came out on to a pleasant turf slope just under the crest of the main range; and on this we found our friends, some fifty or sixty Zulus, squatted in a circle. Not a gun or an assegai was to be seen. So we jumped off and loosened our girths, keeping together, and near the horses, while we went up to the Zulus and commenced a chat.

Among the whole was only one "ring-man" or chief—the rest were pleasant-looking youths, full of smiles and curiosity. Several sat with their arms round each other's necks; all were quite naked, except the "*moucha*" of black-and-white skin. It was just such a scene as the books on South African travel have given us by scores; but it was none the less interesting, now that we saw it in life and sunshine. Most of the youths admitted to have fought at Ulundi; many had been present at Kambula or

Etshowe.

When I asked them if they wanted to go on with the war, they shook their heads and said, grinning broadly, "No, no; you kill too many of us. It isn't fair."

Another added, "You put iron all round your *laager*, and our bullets struck and fell back. I saw them fall."

"Well, do you want peace?" I went on.

"Yes; of course," burst out half-a-dozen in chorus. "You have beaten us,—that is quite right; now go away!"

On being asked why they did not give up their guns if they wanted peace, they declared that they had none, and that the Zulus fought at Ulundi with sticks only. I excited interest with my pistol, which I pulled out to amuse them; and when I opened the chamber and let the six bullets fall into my hand, telling them that I could kill as many Zulus as there were bullets, they took it as a capital joke, and laughed till they woke the echoes.

We persuaded them with difficulty to give us a fresh guide, and then started off for the little nick, now close to us. As we expected, a charming and extensive panorama lay below. At our feet lay the valley of the Umlatoosi, with the river flowing in the centre. Our feet rested on the softest turf; immediately below, the mountain-side fell down, rugged and stone-strewn, dotted with clumps of mimosa, aloes, and cactus. The grass, in patches, was so high that it reached over our heads as we rode through. On the pass we had left perched the Zulus in a well-grouped picture. Beyond the river was a belt of bush thicker than on our side, which reached up to a table-land covered with yellow grass, and stretching for miles, till it ended in a low range of hills, dotted with clumps of trees, park-like in their arrangement, amongst which was our goal, Etshowe. The path, utterly stony, led down at an angle which would have puzzled most horses, and made our own sure-footed little beasts stop frequently to gather up their legs. The descent could not have been less than 2500 feet, and grew steeper the nearer we got to the bottom.

Arrived at last, safe and sound, we came upon a *kraal*, its head-man fearfully wrinkled, surrounded by a dozen younger fellows, who good-naturedly volunteered to show us the way to the ford across the river, not a hundred yards distant.

Here on an open spit of sand we "off-saddled," to give the horses a roll and a feed, while we lit a fire and boiled some coffee. Every movement was watched intently by the Zulus, who squatted near in a circle. A present of tobacco was highly relished, and they went into a tin of Chicago beef with a will. Sardines they spat out with a wry face; and one hulking fellow, with a splendid set of ivories, got rid of a biscuit in the long grass when he thought we were not looking, saying, when detected, that his teeth were not strong enough for that kind of bread. Tea they did not like; but then it was made of a preparation compressed into cakes with milk and sugar, and proved a most nasty imposition.

The valley we lunched in was narrow, shut in with hills and bush. In the middle the river, some twenty yards broad, and only as many inches in depth, rattled over a bed of large pebbles, between a fringe of reeds. It was a lonely spot to sit in, almost alone with a party of savages who owned to have been present at the cutting of our troops' throats not a fortnight previously.

They told us they had seen a white man on this same road once before, when a trader came up, his goods carried on men's heads.

"That was before the fights," one went on. "You English are brave people: you fight us, and beat us—and then you come along the road here by yourselves: you are not afraid, and we like you for it."

It was past one o'clock, and as yet we were but half-way, so we splashed across the river, bidding our Zulu friends good-bye, and soon were lost in the thick bush which covered the opposite bank.

At once we were transported into a new country. Semi-tropical vegetation was all around,—orchids clung to the trees, and let down their roots in dangling ropes; cacti and euphorbias, strangely branched, flung their weird arms across the sky. The ground was choked with undergrowth. Aloes stood stiffly, holding aloft flowers, like flames, coloured scarlet, yellow, and orange. Wild citrons hung on the branches in clusters. Grasses, taller than the trees, stood up sturdily in places, as if to bend was not in their nature; everywhere the flat-topped mimosa-bushes, like big umbrellas, were scattered broadcasts

Through this wilderness the path led, over boulders piled into steps, under branches stuck over with prickles, until it reached the plateau some two miles from the river, and gave us breathing space.

Mile after mile we toiled through a sea of grass—the low hills dotted with forest-trees, to which we were bound, seeming to be as far off as ever. In front still trotted the two guides, —the lad last obtained lithe and active as a deer; the man lounging back at times to beg off, with signs that he was tired, and wanted to go home—all to no use.

Again the scene changed, and the plateau shrouded in long grass gave place to a plain-like valley, its bright surface one great meadow, mapped out with streams and their fringe of reeds, which went about from one clump of forest-trees to another. Herds of pretty Zulu cattle, not unlike Alderneys, were feeding about. *Kraals* surrounded by a stout stockade of branches, began to be plentiful; now and then a partridge or a "coran" got up under foot.

The valley was circular, perhaps ten miles across, entirely closed in by low hills, fringed in places with big trees. On the banks of one of the streams, we came upon a young Zulu girl bathing, who, directly she saw us, hastily tucked a bit of blue rag round her waist, and fled like a deer to her *kraal*, leaving her water-gourds on the ground. These our youngest Zulu guide picked up, taking them with him up to the *kraal* in which she had disappeared, and himself disappearing in turn with a mighty gallant air. The small attention was evidently pleasing to the maiden; for when we got him out again, he stepped very high, smiling grandly, and showing us a handful of some queer eatables which she had given him.

All this time evening was growing apace, and no camp was

to be seen. Mile upon mile we went, our horses stumbling along in the grass, too weary to look out for the ant-bear holes, till we pretty well gave up the search, and looked about for a convenient spot to camp out in.

But the guides kept on, and always pointed ahead, so we left it to them: as long as it was light enough to see the track, we would follow—darkness alone should bring us to a stand-still.

The last glimmer of daylight was dying out over the western hills, when the lads gave a shout and pointed to a tiny light twinkling in the distance, and a row of tents standing near, white and just visible against the sky.

Needless to say we kicked our horses into the feeblest of canters, and went for the welcome sight.

Darker and darker grew the night, the ground got more broken, the road dipping all at once into a hollow, with dark patches of water-weeds coming up to meet us. Just then we came on a *kraal* with its groups sitting outside the huts. There was nothing for it but to single out one of the most talkative, separate him from the rest, and take him nolens volens to show the road. In vain he dodged right and left; we were too quick for him. He flung up his arms, and cried out that the road was as straight as a die—all to no use. He took to taunting us, shouting back, "I shall come back again, for I know my way." "All right, old fellow; very glad to hear you say so," was all the answer he got. Still onwards he was urged in front of our stumbling horses; now crossing a sedge-grown stream on beds of reeds, which squelched under foot; again crawling up banks slippery with moisture and recent cattle-tracks; over stretches of veldt, or through dark clumps of trees, till all of a sudden the fires of a camp burnt up in front, and we heard the welcome sound of the picket as the men challenged us. A bit more, and we were received by a group of dark forms drawn up, with bayonets fixed, who, in answer to our question, "Whose camp's this?" said in the well-known tones of old Ireland.—

"The camp of the 88th Connaught Rangers, sir!"

Our long, tedious ride was over.

Chapter Sixteen
Cetewayo

The Umlalazi, which we had struck, winds between banks turfed with the greenest sward, and brilliant with wild-flowers; now hiding itself in tall reeds or under clumps of magnificent trees; again lying in a silent pool under a rock-terrace verdant with ferns.

Some three miles south was the fort of Etshowe. Its approach is across meadow-land, fairly level, and dotted with groups of trees.

The fort consists of a strong earthen parapet and deeply-cut ditch, enclosing the church and mission station. One end is ornamented with a row of blue-gum trees. Everything else the Zulus had destroyed. The church was pulled down; the houses had been wrecked and burnt; and the parapet, wherever possible, defaced. In the centre of the fort was a railing surrounding a couple of crosses,—one in stone to the memory of a missionary's wife killed by a fall from a waggon; the other in wood over a private in "The Buffs" killed in action.

Outside was the cemetery, enclosed by a neat palisade, and containing about thirty more graves. Beside the fort ran a stream—once shaded by forest-trees, now cut down—the water still lying in pools made by the garrison for bathing. Farther away was the signal-hill from whence messages were flashed across the Tugela by means of the most primitive heliograph. In front of all lay the sea, on that day looking leaden and uninviting. Still it was the sea, and on it lay our road home; so we gazed at it with pleasure, and longed for the day when we should see it closer still.

Wooden musket-racks stood mouldering along the parapet; blindages of cord hung across the embrasures; galleries which had led into the ditch were falling in; the drawbridge at the main entrance creaked and shook as we went across; while four waggons stood deserted in front. Beyond all, the wire entanglements hung from their posts like cobwebs; everything was decaying or destroyed.

On my return to camp I heard a voice which called out, "Pat, fetch me a drink of water."

"Is it out of the basin, sir, I'm to take it?" asked Pat, with a brogue; "because it looks as if some one had washed in it—and it's a bit soiled!"

The road which leads past Etshowe towards the interior was as broad as a turnpike-road in England, by far the best in Zululand. Soon after leaving Etshowe it crosses the wooded hills which enclose the southern side of the Umlatoosi valley, and runs along their crest for some distance parallel to the river. The valley, here ten miles in width, was covered with white grass, dotted with tree-clumps or patches of forest. *Kraals* were perched about in abundance.

To the north of the valley rises a solid wall of mountains, bold, naked, and seemingly impassable. On the very top and away to the right, we could just make out the tents of the Flying Column round St Paul's; but how we were to climb up to them was a puzzle.

On the banks of the river, over which a party of sappers was constructing a foot-bridge, a conductor had just killed a boa-constrictor which measured fourteen feet, and was hideous in proportion. In his palmy days Cetewayo used to preserve the game in this valley as an inducement to white men visiting him to go on farther. Buffalo were plentiful, and several had been shot by officers from St Paul's; while the spoor of eland and koodoo were abundant on the river-bank.

As we rode along I saw the grass by the wayside tossing as if some wild animal was moving about, and going into the place, found that it was caused by an ox in the last extremity of pain. From its back the skin had been torn in a large oval, evidently by the natives, who wanted it for a shield, and did not care to wait till life was extinct. A shot from my revolver put an end to its misery. After crossing the valley we wound under the high cliff on which the tents were pitched. Against its face clung ferns and climbing-plants; below were forest-trees thickly planted and matted together with creepers. Then we turned a corner and commenced the ascent, made just practicable and no more by the Engineers. However, waggons did go up and down; so it must be better than it looked, or oxen in Africa must be most wonderful climbers.

From the top the valley looked like a whitey-brown sea, across which the shadows were playing. Everywhere trees were dotted, now singly, now in groups. Towards the east the valley widened out to meet a grey haze hiding everything—that haze was the Indian Ocean.

On my return to the Division on the Upoko, I found it in every stage of disintegration. The sick had been taken down to Ladysmith under escort of one of the corps. Another had joined the column which was to return to Ulundi, there to dictate peace to our late enemies; while a flying force under Baker Russell was got together to explore and subjugate the northern part of the land. The component parts of this last column came from all about. From St Paul's came the Irregulars, the debris of Buller's cavalry; from Kwamagwasa came two companies of the 94th, the rest of the regiment having already gone on to recommence the old familiar game of fort-building. From Conference Hill came the King's Dragoons, with some Native Contingent brought back, grumbling terribly, from any place where they could be picked up.

We now had to suffer from the excessive liveliness of our new brooms—a disadvantage which must occur after a change of generals, such as we now underwent.

To us ragged ones, whose clothes were greasy and threadbare by four months' exposure, rain-spotted, mud-splashed, and crumpled into ill-looking folds by continual sleeping inside them, appeared many gaily-dressed young men, beautiful in staff dress, hung round with every appliance slung to straps like the wheel-harness of our artillery horses, well shaved, scented, with white cuffs and collars. The apparition accosts us jauntily, and introduces itself as So-and-so, sent on to show us how to do what had been previously left undone; and it soon was plain that the Zulu War had just begun.

The toil, the march, the dragging of waggons, the incessant watchfulness, the long days and sleepless nights; the pickets, when dew or rain wetted you through hours of darkness till dawn crystallised the drops into frost; the bullets which whistled; the silent faces, upturned, hurried into a grave,— these were things which might have happened, but were really of little consequence, now the war had commenced in earnest. This disposition had been made, the other had been arranged, everything would soon be put to rights, and the war so happily inaugurated would soon be brought to a successful termination.

The old oxen which have dragged us for many a mile to the tune of the lash are yoked to again, and set off drowsily to the well-known music; the gaily-appointed new-comers ride ahead on their brand-new chargers, and survey the country with all the interest so novel a sight produces, all the time wondering why the soldiers in rear don't keep up a little better, or omit to strike up a song. There is nothing takes the singing out of a man so much as a dusty road he knows by heart, and a pair of boots with the soles dropping out.

But if our spirits were low, our clothes were lower.

"Don't you say 'sir' to an officer in your regiment when he addresses you?" I said to a man of the "King's" who was answering my questions somewhat curtly in the camp.

"Beg your pardon, sir, but I did not know you were an officer," said the man, saluting; and when I looked down on myself I felt the man had the best of it.

Wideawakes with broad brims were much patronised, and were not calculated to add to a military appearance. In the matter of trousers the men displayed the utmost ingenuity. Patches of sheepskin, of bullock-hide, of leather, gunny-bag, the oilcloth lining of bales, nothing came amiss. We used to laugh at the Volunteers; but they had bought suits of new "cords" at the "winkler's" waggon, and were to us as is the Park lounger to the street Arab.

Constantly sleeping in the suit worn during the day had

called up a host of unwelcome strangers. One young officer appeared in a piebald costume, the result of boiling his whole kit to exterminate them.

"Don't come too close," said another, as I made for his bed, the only seat available; "I've got ringworm!"

"Oh," I answered, "I thought you meant the other thing."

"Well, it isn't; but I've had them too," was the reply.

Another, to whom previously the name of the insect had been unknown, was seen to approach his servant holding his tunic at arm's-length, when the following dialogue ensued:—

"Oh yes, sir, it's one of they things the men has."

"What do they do to you; do they bite you?"

"No, sir; they terrifies you."

"What on earth do you mean?"

"Why, sir, they walks up and down you, and terrifies you, till you scratch them off, sir."

Yet in all except this matter of dress our soldiers were twice the men they had been before Ulundi.

I remember some of them came to me previous to that time with a complaint that they had been served out with flour instead of bread or biscuit, and wishing to know what they were to do with it, as at present it was quite useless to them, from their inability to cook. I explained that bread was made from flour, and that the sooner they set to work to make some, the sooner their breakfasts would be ready. My answer was not thought satisfactory, and for a day or two the flour was thrown away. Then the sharper fellows heated ant-hills, and laying the tin lid of a biscuit-box on the top, managed to bake some excellent scones. Others followed; and from that time the issue of flour was hailed with delight, owing to the various ways of cooking it.

Strolling round the cooking-places, I found, later on, a small town had sprung up; the men had copied the Zulus in making a few sticks into a *kraal*, which, thatched with dry grass, made a most comfortable snuggery. At the door began the "broad-arrow" cooking-trench, terminating in a chimney made of old biscuit-boxes, from which the smoke escaped merrily;

the cooks, fine fellows with beards, squatting inside the *kraal*, smoking their pipes and watching the dinners cooking outside, themselves independent of the weather. A few months on, a campaign had taught these bits of experience to men who just previously at Aldershot had found it impossible to cook their potatoes in their skins, though provided with an excellent kitchen-range; "the weather was too frosty."

Everything now was fish in their net. As I walked along a river after a chance wild duck, a couple of soldiers ran up to me with the news that there was "a nice owl in the bushes there, sir." The "nice owl" I presently shot and presented to them; as they said, on departing with the poor bird, "It will be so good in to-morrow's stew!"

The new column under Baker Russell was to rendezvous at Fort Cambridge, a post lately made by the 94th some fifteen miles north of our old road, and a mile or two west of Intabankulu, a noted Zulu stronghold, as yet quite undisturbed. Between it and Fort Cambridge ran the White Umvolosi, crossed lower down by the army before Ulundi. Baker Russell himself was tall and soldier-like, a favourite with every one, and the coveted possessor of a Canadian coat of beaver-skin, admirably suited for the cold mornings which were the prelude of the day's march.

As we were making for the rendezvous, a troop of hartebeests showed about a mile away, and a couple of sportsmen started at once in pursuit. The ground was favourable; and the column having halted for the mid-day meal, was able to watch the whole of the chase. Presently the horsemen dismounted for a shot, and the excitement vented itself in loud cries and directions from the men.

"Keep your head down, captain darlin'!"

"Don't ye see that big one with the two horns; he's a cow, he is, and not a deer at all, at all."

"Holy mother, but them's the pretty creatures to shoot!"

Just then puff went the smoke of the two rifles, and off galloped the hartebeests untouched; the two ponies taking the opportunity of making for camp as hard as they could lay legs to the ground, amid a howl of delight from the spectators.

On nearing Fort Cambridge, under an isolated peak which formed an excellent landmark, called by the Zulus Inyayeni, the column struck the road to Ulundi, by which the advance was originally intended. It was an excellent road, wide and well defined, encumbered by few hills, and altogether better than the one which the army took.

Across the Umvolosi a drift had been cut by the Engineers. Now a drift in South Africa signifies a place where a waggon can get over a river; and experiences of drifts are amongst the most trying of all met with in the land. The banks of its rivers are continually worn away by the stream, and are usually perpendicular. So the angle has to be cut away on either side, the result being a sharp pitch to go down, and another like it to climb. Between the two runs the stream, always rapid, deep or shallow according to the season, its bed sand, soft and easily cut up. You will be lucky also if it is free from mud-holes.

The method of crossing a drift is invariable, and as bad as it can be. The team is tugged at by the "*forelooper*," by a thong of hide fastened to the horns of the leading couple. A good "*forelooper*" circles his team round at first, so as to get a straight pull when their noses are in the right direction; but the boys we had been reduced to pulled any way but the right one, and so the oxen were brought up to the drift in form like the letter S—the waggon they pulled taking the bank at the side and remaining stuck fast. If it escapes this danger and takes the descent fairly, up goes the hind part as the fore-wheels lumber down into the sand; while the driver, ceasing to crack his whip, runs back and screws up a log of wood against the hind-wheels as a break. In consequence, when the waggon reaches the bottom it stops dead, the fore-wheels sink axle-deep, the oxen in every possible attitude in front. Now come fiends armed with long whips, who place themselves on either side of the team, and on a signal, with horrible yells and whistles, crack their whips with the rapidity of lightning against the bullocks' sides. The maddened beasts strain at the "*trek tow*," and if the waggon gives, pull it across. But as often as not the wheels have silted up, and the machine refuses to budge an inch. More whips arrive, the yells redouble, the floggers dance round the oxen ; the poor tortured beasts twist about to escape the blows, some kneel or lie down, others plunge and turn tail foremost in the line, while some get the chain twisted round their legs and are thrown bodily into the stream. A fresh span of sixteen more is brought down and hooked on in front, and the uproar begins again. At the first pull of the double team crack goes the chain, and the new span wanders calmly off, only to be brought back and tackled to again. Meantime cart-loads of stones have been thrown under the wheels, and the long grass and weeds fringing the river have been cut by armfuls and laid on the top.

The drift over the White Umvolosi was as bad as recent rain could make it, and it took half a day to pass over thirty waggons, and as much more to get the tired oxen to a camping-ground barely two miles farther.

Ten miles beyond, Fort George was built, and we sat down in expectation of what the Zulus would do in answer to our proclamation that unless they brought in their arms within four days we should burn their *kraals*.

There were plenty of Zulus about: their villages everywhere were partly inhabited. Intabankulu, the mountain over the fort, was known to be the refuge for some thousands: Cetewayo was at large only thirty miles in front, and the smoke of signal-fires was constantly seen.

The Zulus managed these admirably: a bunch of a certain kind of grass, which, when burnt, gave out a peculiar white smoke, was thrown on the fire,—a white puff followed, and the signal was complete. In the search for Cetewayo, I remember watching about a dozen of these puffs, ascending one after another, in the direction which we were following, until the line was answered, from the very place near which the king was hiding, by a thin column of smoke projected suddenly upwards.

Fort George stood close to a mission station, then in ruins. Some mud-walls and a couple of orange-trees were all that remained of what was once a prosperous settlement. Other stations, also in ruins, were scattered about; and strange tales were told of the missionaries. That the Zulus laughed at them there is little doubt: they were in the habit of preaching in the language which they learnt from books — quite different from that spoken by the natives, who came, as they admitted, to listen to a funny man speaking a funny tongue.

A German missionary purchased two young children, girls, for ten blankets, just as they were going to be killed with their mother, who had been "smelt out" for witchcraft. These girls he educated and brought up as Christians. When they were old enough, he sent them down to Maritzburg to purchase his annual stores. Here one of them took ill and died; whereupon the prudent German, fearing he might lose the second one also, disposed of her on her return to a Zulu for ten cows,—thus clearing a handsome profit on the transaction. Another included in the list of stores he wanted for the year's use a hundredweight of gunpowder. The quantity seemed excessive; and it was broadly hinted that he wanted it to sell again to the Zulus.

"Oh dear, no," said the worthy man: "it is not for that bad purpose I buy it; but my servant shoots some game occasionally for my table, and I buy powder to supply him."

In shape Fort George was like a diamond, with faces some ninety yards long, flanked by a redoubt at either end. These held the hospital, stores, ammunition, and working-tools: the larger enclosure was taken up by the cavalry and artillery, and some mounted irregulars. Baker Russell's camp was pitched outside one of the redoubts, just above the ruins of the mission station, and facing Intabankulu, which towered grandly up some four miles away. The mountain was wooded in parts, and provided with broad shelves, difficult of approach, and thick with Zulus, the smoke from their fires being ever present. Opposite, and fifteen miles south, was Inlhlazatsi, still to be explored; while in the east the N'gome range rose like a wall, marking the course of the Black Umvolosi, about ten miles away. Through the basin thus formed wound a river, laid down on the maps as Enhlongana. Here, forcing its way through beds of reeds, or bubbling over rocks, it tumbled, near the camp, over a shelf 150 feet high, in a graceful cascade. Miles away, on the top of a ridge, were waggons "trekking" to the fort, anon disappearing behind a hill, to appear again on the steep side of a slope which led into the camp. The hills round were dotted with the cavalry horses, and with countless cattle, — some our own, others belonging to the Zulus, whose *kraals* lay scattered far and near. Those to which the Zulus had returned were sacred; but others, deserted by their owners, were brought into camp as firewood—an actual necessity in this treeless land — their segments, like pieces of huge baskets, blackened with age, coming in on the top of a dandified mule-waggon.

Troops of Zulus now began to arrive in answer to our summons, treading invariably one behind the other in Indian file, often hundreds of yards long, according to the number. These brought with them guns and assegais; often herds of pretty cattle, all young bulls, and so little loss to the owners. The guns were a collection of rubbish, mostly from Germany, a few nondescript "big bores," or bigger blunderbusses, with a sprinkling of English double-barrelled guns, invariably damaged.

The men were naked, all but the "*moucha,*" walking magnificently, upright and springy, their skins like satin, their faces far above the usual negro type, and their figures pictures of grace and activity. They came on without the slightest show of fear, straight into the camp, and were taken at once to headquarters, where they all squatted in a semicircle while their arms were collected—each man in turn being called by name, when he advanced and deposited the arms he carried, receiving in return a pass to secure him from being molested. Then a short speech was made: "Cetewayo is no longer king. You will not again be 'smelt out' as witches. You will not be killed; and you can marry the girl you like." The speech was received with grave attention, and evidently relished, as the fellows were unanimous on its conclusion in raising a hand apiece and exclaiming "*Koss!*" in token of assent. In appearance they wonderfully resembled one another: the young men had often really a pleasing expression, which soon assumes an air of cunning as age creeps on. Their eyes were always on the move restlessly round the circle, but not a word was spoken; every one of them was too intent on listening. Deep furrows appear to mark their faces early in life, lending an anxious cast to them. Their hair is worn very short, often shaved, especially on the crown of the head above the "ring."

The recognised leader of each band always sat in the middle of the circle, and was most implicitly obeyed.

One day came Mahanana, a brother of Cetewayo's, and not unlike him in face and form. He was enormously fat, standing over six feet in stature, perfectly naked, all but the "*moucha*," and came forty miles to surrender to us, on foot. His body-guard consisted of six rough-looking Zulus, who squatted with their master opposite the tent-door, as though they were equals. But there was no mistaking the chief; his composure was intense, the indifference with which he treated everything about so delightful, and his whole attitude truly royal. An officer wishing to possess something of his as a memento, asked him to give him the rough stick he carried. Mahanana raised his eyes for a second, and replied in his low, soft voice—

"That stick has touched my hand, and there may be some of my own royal sweat upon it. I am a king, and nothing of a king's can touch a stranger and not be defiled!" The officer, foiled about the stick, asked for the tiny snuffbox he carried in his ear. Without a word the Zulu raised his hand and took it out, with hardly a motion of his body; then held it out, and let the little bit of horn drop into the Englishman's hand. The latter, in return, brought out some sticks of tobacco and a couple of boxes of matches, both "worth their weight in gold in a Zulu's eyes, and offered them to Mahanana. He quietly held out one hand, and as the present fell into his palm, just passed it over to his follower sitting next to him, as if the things were utterly beneath his notice. And yet the man was a prisoner, and beaten. It is amusing to talk to the Zulus; they are so magnificent in their ignorance, and so full of their own superiority.

Riding at a hand-gallop along the plateau connecting Inlhlazatsi with Fort George, a big fellow joined me, and ran alongside for some five miles. His tongue never stopped. Much that he said was unintelligible, and a great deal was pure brag, with simple begging for tobacco thrown in.

"Oh yes," he said; "I was at Ulundi, and tried to kill you. If you had run away, we would have killed every one; but you didn't. Myself and three friends determined to get nearer to your guns than any other Zulu ; and we did "—three or four men actually got within thirty yards of one face of the square, "Then my three friends were killed,—pouf—pouf— pouf'—and he imitated the bullets whistling, and his head bobbing,—"so I ran away; but you had put iron palings in front of your men, and hung red coats on them, so that our guns could not kill them. I saw myself the bullets fall off them." Every one said this same thing; it was only that which beat them. "Yes, yes; you have beaten us, and now you are masters of all people. No one can fight against any one who can beat the Zulus. How can we fight men who wear boots like that?"—pointing to my riding-boots. "We can't wear such boots: and then you put boots on your horses. Who can fight such clever people? Can you give me tobacco?" To get on with them, a great thing is to observe their social customs. To visit their *kraal*, etiquette is necessary. You ride into the centre of the huts without a sign. Out will crawl one or more "ring-men," perhaps a naked urchin will bolt after them; in the hole they have crept through will be a suspicion of keen eyes watching you. The chiefs come round you, and, after an interval, say—

"Have you ridden far?"

"Yes, many miles."

Then follows silence, during which the eyes inside the *kraals* become visible and impatient; so the chief goes on—

"In this country the crops are bad, and we are hard pressed."

There being no answer required, we only nod.

"In Natal you gather mealies in waggons. That is a rich country. "Why do you come to this poor country?"

"I come to see it—nothing else."

"Give me some tobacco."

"Yes, here is some."

"Well, 'thaka-boma'—good day!" and the ceremony is complete. You are a friend, and cordiality is established. The watching eyes prove to be those of the women, who crawl outside, and giggle and chatter out of arm's-length, their husbands sometimes dragging one forward by her outstretched hand, amid the jeers of her comrades, to receive tobacco. The children watch you farther off still, and you are soon in the midst of all the family grievances.

Chapter Seventeen
Zulus

Did you ever see a fire which extended for twenty miles? Such a fire we saw at Fort George, and the spectacle was not uncommon. It began on the White Umvolosi, advancing on a front of half-a-dozen miles, till it ran up the valley on the far side of Intabankulu; it licked up the grass from that mountain, creeping up its slopes to windward, and eating down the ravines and hollows sheltered from the breeze; it roared across the flats where the Zulus were hiding their cattle, and put itself out on the banks of the Black Umvolosi, twenty miles from its starting-point. For days its flames were slowly lapping against the wind.

All caused by a match thrown carelessly away, or a waggon-driver's fire of cow-dung. Fortunately the damage does good, and in a month's time the blackened ground will be green again, and gemmed with flowers.

But for all that we feared the fires, and used to burn a belt round ourselves,—for we were breast-high in a sea of yellow grass, as dry as tinder, in which a spark meant a conflagration. These grass-fires near camp came to be well understood; and as soon as one occurred, every man used to turn out, provided with a blanket or tentpeg-bag, and set to work to beat it out. If the wind was high the fire beat them, and those who were not careful got badly scorched: nothing was able to stop the fury of the flames, —they rushed onwards like a wave, amid much crackling, driving before them men and cattle. Dense volumes of smoke roll in front, and the flaming circle sweeps on as fast as a horse can canter. So rapid is the pace that the ground behind is strewn with half-burnt grass; while many of the more fleshy leaves survive, and dot the blackened plain with green spots.

Inlhlazatsi is a remarkable mass of granite, terraced and flat-topped. It was the bad reputation given to this mountain which turned our column off the road to Ulundi—a story, like many others in South Africa, much exaggerated. It is put down on the map as the Green Stone Mountain—Inlhlaza signifying "green:" the more probable meaning is "angular"—the Zulu word for that term and the colour being identical.

And very angular it is—the edges sharp as knives, the descents bold and clearly defined: it is circled by terraces of naked rock; and the top is as flat as a table, sticking up some 6000 feet above the sea. It was with a feeling of awe that we approached a mountain, so long looked at from a distance, enveloped in doubt and mystery, and able to turn an army. Round its base were kraals, with cattle feeding and Zulus tending them, who, when addressed, answered volubly enough. Near one village were the remains of a waggon,—doubtless dragged thus far after Isandlwana.

The fearless bearing of the men was hardly borne out by that of two young girls whom we came upon all of a sudden. Dropping their bundles of firewood, they took to their heels, and ran like antelopes, till we headed them off and made signs that no harm was intended. But fear was on their faces, and they refused all consolation, while they wrung their hands and looked about vainly for escape,—the younger and more buxom of the two, in an agony of despair, flinging her shapely arms over her head and crying out, "O Lord! it's come at last!"

Very few unmarried girls were met with: we had an evil character amongst the people, and they hid their women—their most valuable property—in the caves,—a rough life for the poor little "Intombie." Ten cows are the lowest price for a girl; and thirty cows give a man the right to be called a chief, and make other people do his work; so "Intombies" are a valuable property.

A chief called Mahobolin, and a friend of his Manyonyoba — pestilent fellows, living on the Pongola, the extreme northern boundary of Zululand—about this time began to be troublesome. To them we had sent a messenger offering the same terms as had been given to others. Mahobolin replied that he only refrained from killing our messenger because he wanted him to come back and tell us that he would see us further first.

So orders were issued to march against him. This continual cropping up of the war in fresh places was very wearisome. In war you go on till you smash your enemy or he smashes you. With us, we were always beginning again just as we had finished. It was against our feelings to live amongst the people —to ride about alone many miles from camp—to visit their *kraals*, and laugh and talk with them,—when at any minute we might be burning and killing, as in the early days when Isandlwana was unavenged.

The daily routine too, fearfully monotonous, offered no relief. The country was cursed with a fatal sameness, reflecting itself on the imagination. Mile after mile was crossed; in front a low line of hill, beyond which you may expect a view over a fresh bit of country. It is miles away, and you rise in your stirrups to catch the welcome view, only to be disappointed; it is just another stretch of grass, interminable. Distant mountains there are, but they seldom get nearer, and when they do, dwindle dreadfully.

Every valley is a network of dongas, and most of the hill-tops are paved with boulders.

Such was Zululand to us.

But there are rivers which dance over the shingle as merrily as any English trout-stream; and miles of turf on mountain-tops where the cattle group themselves; and clouds, fleecy white, against the blue; and sunshine lavished everywhere.

Give us peace, a bed, a few books, and meals unassociated with the trek-ox, served on a decent plate, and Zululand would be as good a station as any down in the army-list.

It was Sunday morning when we left Fort George, just a fortnight after we had made it, and started for a trip of some seventy miles towards the north. We cross the Umvolosi at our former drift, now worn hard by constant traffic, and camp on the right bank, while the interpreter goes off to talk to Sikitwayo, the chief of the district, and somewhat disposed to give trouble.

He was old, he said, too feeble to come to us, and with no force at his command strong enough to make his tribe come in. On our paying him a visit he had bolted in a fright, his men somewhat inclined to show fight, especially when we walked off with three hundred of their cattle as hostages. The argument gained the day; and he sent word to say he was in a *kraal* near the column, with a number of guns, and his share of the cattle taken at Isandlwana. These presently arrived, his own were restored, and a pass given to him and his tribe.

Chapter Eighteen
The Troublesome Chiefs

In fog and drizzle we left the Umvolosi, and marched up a valley west of the Umyati range till we struck the river again, twenty miles above our first point, and under a quaintly-shaped hill, which stuck out of the plain, and is called Inseke.

The ground about was historic—the scene of Wood's early skirmishes. His camping-grounds were about. Opposite our own was the one he occupied when the intelligence of Isandlwana made him leave faster than he came. Everywhere the oats springing up in rows betrayed the old horse-lines. Bundles of firewood, drifts nearly washed out, and tumble-down parapets, marked the way he went. Due west, and exactly behind us, was the top of Bemba's Kop, near Conference Hill. North of that was Kambula, a dozen miles away; and in front, a little less, Zlobane, the mountain which still hid on its slopes the relics of its ill-fated day.

As the troublesome chiefs we had come to look up lived under the shadow of this hill, it was thought wise to send out a party to see what they were about, before the main body proceeded to business.

The reconnaissance consisted entirely of mounted men: a squadron of the King's Dragoon Guards, all young men, stoutly made, who always managed to keep their clothes in capital order—their horses a little tucked up, many bought in Natal, but all round fairly fit; another of Mounted Infantry, dressed in red-serge coats, brown cord-breeches, helmets, and ankle-boots —a most serviceable and useful contingent; Darcy, who escaped by a miracle from Zlobane, brought his Frontier Light Horse, rough-and-ready fellows, with slung carbines, and ever-lasting pipes; Lonsdale's Horse, the same in every respect except that they were fewer, and wore blue round their hats instead of red; and last, though not the worst by far, a party of Natal Mounted

Police, if anything the pride of our colonial soldiers. Our flank was guarded by some rough-looking natives, mounted too, the contribution of a chief named Tetelika.

Sometimes the track led across patches of Tambouky grass, coming over our horses' heads, or through mealie-fields, long since picked. Close by was sure to be a *kraal*, its occupants looking rather doubtful of our intentions. Often we stumbled across an old cattle-*kraal*, its stones hidden in the grass, by no means pleasant to ride among. But the most part of our way was across the rolls of land which slid away from a range on the right, and which were then emerald with spring grass. Arrived on the bank of a stream, we off-saddled, while some neighbouring *kraals* were looked to. Tin pots were unfastened, armfuls of mealie-stalks brought in, and coffee boiled. This, with Chicago beef, was our dinner and supper in one. The horses were watered, and picketed in a hollow square, and preparations made ostensibly for the night. But when the stars shone out, the saddles were put on again, and the men mounting in silence, we trooped off to the real halting-place.

This we found a couple of miles away on the side of a bare hill. Cold and damp with the fast-falling dew, we got down. Blankets were unstrapped, the horses tied together by a rope running through their snaffles, in colonial parlance called "ringing;" no saddles were removed. Silently the men rolled themselves in their blanket and waterproof sheet, and lay down by their horses. The hillside looked like a field of battle, when all the dead lie swathed, awaiting burial.

So in cold and damp we passed the night, our faces turned up to the stars, the hard ground like iron every way we lay. Men snoring, horses whinnying, a distant dog barking; and in the fog creeping up from the valley the groups on sentry looking big and ghostly, fancy, aided by drowsiness, lending to them a dozen different disguises. The long night drags away, and at the first streak of grey in the east every one rouses out, nose-bags are put on the horses, blankets rolled, and a sharp walk taken to keep the blood from stagnation. The horses fed, and we mount and away, meeting the chill morning air till the sun tints the hill-tops with, rosy-red, and a stream convenient for the morning's coffee is picked out. Such was one of many amongst the nights we spent in Zululand.

In front was the Zlobane, black and gloomy, with the sun rising behind it. To our left was the Zinguin range, and Zinguin's Nek, or Pass, towards the Zlobane.

Filing along we came upon a skeleton in the long grass, then another, the bones bleached white, a few fragments of hair alone remaining; we were crossing the track which the poor hunted wretches took on that fatal 28th of March.

Its tale has been already told.

Wood receiving orders to make a diversion at the same time as the relief of Etshowe was contemplated, thought of the Zlobane. He had been there before; it lay handy to Kambula, was known to be rich in cattle, and as yet had been only partially ravaged. So Buller, with a large force of Irregulars, went out to try what he could do.

The night before the attack he camped under the hill, starting before daybreak the next morning, so as to be at the top about dawn and surprise the natives. The way lay up the south-eastern corner, that furthest removed from the rest of the troops at Kambula. A fog favoured the ascent, and the men got up without being seen, and drove off a large quantity of cattle. Then they off-saddled on the flat summit of the hill for breakfast.

But the fog which had favoured their own attack had also allowed an army of Zulus, some 20,000 strong, advancing against Kambula, to come up unseen. From the mountain-top our men saw this vast army close below, the main body making up the spur which they had just climbed, the two "horns" circling round either side of the base. These advanced at a run, twenty men in breadth; the track they made, forty feet wide, was plain enough even then, five months after they had stamped it out by their feet. A general rush was made for the end of the mountain nearest to the line of retreat. In that direction the plateau on which our horsemen were, drew in to a very narrow neck, connecting it with a lower plateau a mile in length, which formed the western half of the Zlobane. The part on which they rode was surrounded by sides scarped perpendicularly out of the rock, and was a couple of hundred feet higher than the western plateau. This difference of level was joined at the narrowest point by an awfully steep slope of loose boulders, piled together any way; on either side a sheer precipice. And to this neck the fugitives made, hard pressed in rear by the Zulus.

How any got down is a miracle. The place is hardly practicable on foot; on a horse, or even leading one, the descent was doubly difficult; and those who made for it knew only too well that to lose one's horse was to lose one's life.

It was here Piet Uys lost his life and Buller won the Cross. A cruel slaughter took place, those who escaped it here meeting it further down where the "horns" had come and waited for them. Only those mounted well got away, and they were few enough.

There were thus many places at which danger was met: on the eastern plateau, where the Zulus first swarmed, aided by the inhabitants; at the descent to the western plateau, where the larger number were killed; on this second plateau, where were scattered Zulus prowling; on the long and steep side of the mountain itself, which must be faced ere the plain below is reached, then full of savages; and lastly, on the long homeward ride to Kambula, followed for many a mile by the ever-active Zulus, and met at every turn by sneaking villagers.

On the crest of the narrow neck we found numerous skeletons, many a good deal broken up, probably by the monkeys; on the lower plateau were a few; and at the base of the mountain they lay thickly enough in a broad line, gradually getting thinner, till only detached bones were met, these extending for three miles from the actual mountain. All were perfect skeletons, the rags hanging here and there about them; some with the hair still attached to the scalp. Weatherly was recognised by his long fair moustache lying by his side, and the skeleton of a boy, his son, not many yards from him. We gave them what burial we could, and paid the last marks of respect to our soldiers' graves.

The directing spirit of all this disaster, Unsebe, the chief of the Zlobane, gave himself up to us soon after we arrived.

He was a spare, miserable-looking creature, undersized, and wore a dirty railway-rug of a huge chess-board pattern as his only garment. His followers, of whom fifty were with him, were cruel-looking savages, anything but pleased at the turn things had taken. Amongst the whole there was not a spark of human feeling; hard faces, deep-lined foreheads, beetling brows, and noses low and squat, they were of all others ready to gloat over the agonies of a wretch unhappy enough to fall alive into their power.

Every Zulu carries, generally in his hair, a bone scraper, to remove the perspiration from his face and body; they also carry snuff-boxes in their ears. Snuff is a passion with them; they will sit the whole day talking and snuffing. They talk differently from other Africans, seldom raising their voices above an earnest whisper.

One evening came in the news of the capture of Cetewayo, and the men cheered lustily, the poor ragged fellows out at knees and elbows thinking that the war was over, and nothing remained but to go home and spend their savings. The orderly camp was transformed into a scene of noisy rejoicing; Baker Russell and the staff brought out the last case of champagne. At the fourth bottle the colonels were asked in; at the fifth a glass of grog for the men was ordered all round; at the sixth a message was sent to release a prisoner lying under sentence of the "cat" on the morrow.

Every one was pleased at Marter's good fortune; personally, on account of his general popularity—and generally, that the 2nd Division had finished the war without the assistance of the new-comers.

Marter had much trouble with his guides, who refused to show him the way, saying, when pressed, "the wind blows from the east;" "the trees all bend to the south-east."

Arriving at the *kraal* at last, he saw a very fat Zulu lying inside the door, whom at first he mistook to be the king. On entering, Cetewayo came up and demanded who he was. Marter replied that he was an officer sent to capture him. Cetewayo said, "I only surrender to a chief." And on Marter explaining that his rank was that of chief, the king surrendered at once.

He was a man of enormous proportions, his thighs stupendous. After a time he complained of being tired, and a horse was prepared for him by taking off the holsters and making the saddle as large as possible. But he turned surly, and refused to ride; whereupon he was told if he would not walk or ride, he must be strapped across the saddle. The threat succeeded, and he set off walking once more. For forty-eight hours he refused food, though a bullock was given him to kill as he pleased: he said he was afraid of poison. At last hunger conquered, and the bullock was killed and eaten. Then he walked quietly along till the camp was reached. No reception was afforded him: he was marched to the tent assigned, and as soon as possible sent off under escort. So ended an eventful history.

The tribe hereabouts was the Makulusin, one of the most warlike of the whole, claiming the royal line, and so ever foremost in the fighting, and always ready to begin again. Five thousand of these warriors were reported to be under arms in front waiting for us, anxious for a fight. A party of them had descended from Zinguin's Nek, and carried off some of our cattle only a few miles from camp. On the day following, I happened to be out some miles towards the front, accompanied by an escort, when we met a Zulu youth tending some cattle, who, as soon as he saw us, started at a run for us, smiling broadly, and telling us he could show us where yesterday's thieves were.

"And you will fight them, won't you? What fun! I shall come too and look on. That's the place, up there in the bush. If you go on, they will begin to shoot, and you will shoot too. I will stop here myself; I don't care to go any closer, for I don't want to be killed!"

However, he was disappointed of the fight, as the fellows had left, sending in to camp the stolen cattle. A little farther on we saw two Zulus running to meet us: they proved to be head-men anxious to make submission and save their *kraals*,—one of them saying his people had a flock of 400 sheep which they had taken from the Dutch early in the war, and now wished to return. So we sent him off for the sheep, and drove them back to camp—lean, ragged creatures, wild as hawks, and fleet as race-horses. During our stay the Engineers had put up a small fort called Piet Uys, and had just completed it when the sheep arrived; so as no other place was available, it was thought best to let them pass the night inside, and they were driven in accordingly. But confinement was not a habit with them of late: the four earthen walls all round them appeared strange, and they stood looking at them in a lump, evidently much disturbed in their minds. All at once the bell-wether gave a start: he separated himself from the herd at a bound, and with another cleared the parapet in front, the rest following with a mighty rush, under which the beautiful parapet gave way, and Fort Piet Uys was a ruin.

Our young guide turned out so useful that we persuaded him to stay with us. This he seemed quite pleased with, but changed his mind later, and said he would go back to his *kraal*. We told him he should be well treated at the camp, but he still demurred, running beside our horses when we cantered as easily as he did when they walked. At last we wanted to decide it one way or another whether he would come or go, and put the question to him point-blank.

"Well, I have not made up my mind yet," said the independent young fellow, who never saw for a moment how completely he was in our power.

Our fight evaporated altogether on our marching to meet it, and the villagers received us with smiles instead of assegais. The much-boasting Mahobolin gave himself up, and only Manyonyoba was left: that he would fight was pretty certain, as he had been attacked unsuccessfully several times owing to the caves he lived in; and he knew, moreover, if he did surrender, that he was to be treated as a criminal.

To get to him a road had to be found or made. A Zulu was impressed from the nearest *kraal*, and told to lead us to a certain mountain which lies in the direction we want to go. This he at first refuses, professing ignorance. Persuasive measures alter his tone, and he sets out along a foot-track, crossed by many others just like it, and each as distinct as the other. He motions you to follow, and starts off at a trot. Streams, gullies, dongas, and stony hills he passes with the assurance that over there is the road and nowhere else. The Sappers set to work; drifts are cut, bog-holes filled in, *dongas* turned, and next morning you see the waggons following your steps, leaving an excellently-marked road behind them.

In this way we reached the Bevano river, climbed the slopes of the Dumbe Mountain, left Makatees Kop on the left, and finally reached the Pongola some five miles below Luneberg.

And the change after Zululand was pleasant. Farms, in ruins certainly, dotted the land, the blue-gum trees about them untouched. Wild-flowers lent colour to the rolling uplands; petunias, lobelias, auriculas, daisies, dielytras, marigolds, zinnias, hyacinths, and orchids were blooming everywhere. Among the rest a snowdrop reminded us pleasantly of home.

The slopes were absolutely covered with anthills—so thick that the difficulty was to find a clear place for the camp. In many, bees had turned out the ants, making their own nest inside, and a hunt was always going on to track the bees flying homewards to the ant-hill in which the honey was. Altogether the ants have a sore time of it; the ant-bear licks them up by thousands; the soldier burns them alive in their nest, turned into an oven; and the bees hustle them out to put their honey in their place.

The country north of the Pongola is mountainous and broken; here and there are flat-topped hills with precipitous sides. Patches of bush climb the slopes, and flowering-trees are scattered amongst grey boulders. These slopes are honeycombed with crevices leading past the boulders into caves, and have for ages formed a sanctuary for bands of robbers, their chief at that time Manyonyoba.

We pitched our camp on a slope running down to the Intombie river, not a hundred yards from the scene of the disaster the previous March. The trenches where the tents stood still remained; littered papers, empty tins of preserved-meat, and other rubbish, strewed the ground. On the river's bank were two mounds under which lay the dead. The skeletons of two soldiers were still unburied; the poor fellows had been killed while running in the long grass, and that burnt, their bones were exposed. The bodies of two natives were found in a ditch, locked tightly in each other's arms—the one a Zulu, the other one of our own people. Farther on lay the skeleton of the horse shot under an officer when employed in reconnoitring with Commandant Shermbrucker, the two escaping on the latter's horse; while the third, a German orderly, was killed.

Here, too, were the remains of Meyer's mission station, once a large thriving settlement; then destroyed, and its name made hideous by the cruelties practised on the poor Kafirs who happened to be caught there by Manyonyoba. Roses bloomed in the hedges; peach-trees were white with flower; figs, plums, and apricots were forming, and mulberries were already ripe.

Beyond the Intombie the mountains close in on either side of the road to Derby. On the right a huge flat-topped giant formed the stronghold of Umbeline, then killed, but notorious for his savage deeds, more especially that enacted on the Intombie. On the left, and on either side of the river, extending up its course for six miles or more, were the caves we had come to rout out. Thousands of ant-hills, bright red, covered the valley; two hideous dongas, almost impassable, straggled across it; in the distance a ruined farm stood out with melancholy significance. The day before, Tetelika's Natives, at a parley with the robbers who lived in the caves nearest to our camp, had persuaded them by fair words to come out of their hiding-place, and had then treacherously murdered eight of them, the rest flying in every direction. We had hoped to induce these people to surrender as others had done, but this incident put a stop to all, and nothing was left but brute force. So the 94th, with the Light Horse and Mounted Infantry, set off for the mountain. The King's Dragoon Guards skirted the base: the Irregulars made their way far round and closed the road in that direction; while the Infantry, in single file, led straight up the mountain for the caves. The sun blazed with intense heat on the boulders and tall grass which strewed the way. The *dongas* were crossed by paths so steep as to bring us to hands and feet. The red dust rose in clouds. In a mealie-field we came on the body of one of the Zulus killed yesterday, stuck in a hole in a sitting position. Above the shelf which we followed, rose a wall of broken stone, almost a precipice, studded with bushes and long grass. High up the black entrances to the caves looked out, and every movement of the leaves which partly concealed them might be a Zulu. Against these the soldiers were sent to scramble over the rough ground, and to take up a position on the ridge above. It was a stiff climb, pretty enough to watch—the red coats dodging in and out, half hidden by the undergrowth, till they perched themselves on the highest points. The path went up a steep ascent to a second shelf; then came another stiff pull, and the thick bush in front of the principal caves was reached. The trees had been fired by the Zulus as we came up, and the place was in a blaze. Cactus and euphorbia gave a pleasant shade to the courtyards which lay about. Advantage had been taken of the rocks to lay out these little circles: wherever the boulders did not divide them, a low wall had been built. Each courtyard had its own neatly-made *kraal*.

It was a picturesque place, most difficult to take if defended by resolute men. Everywhere the blocks of stone left openings which led within: some great holes; others nothing more than crevices,—all shown to be in constant use by the well-worn paths which led to them.

On all sides lay the proceeds of robberies. Goats bleated inside; chickens just now pursued by stray men; huge straw-baskets of mealies, the best of the very best description; a copper-boiler torn bodily away from the brickwork; a mealie-mill; a grindstone; some carpenter's tools; beams; portions of doors and windows; a 7-pounder shell; and a litter of puppies.

Knots of soldiers watched the holes, and natives searched the crevices. Above all, the fire crackled, covering up the earth with ashes. The spaces between the boulders had got filled up with black powder, the debris of the burning rubbish, and it required the greatest care to prevent stepping on it and getting smothered. Just then we heard a shot, followed by a shout, and a native falls wounded with an assegai through his thigh; a Zulu had plugged him unseen from a hole. The place was like a rabbit-warren in which the enemy are unseen, while we stand out plain and distinct.

Nothing could be done by ordinary means, so the wood, mats, mealies, and other combustibles were piled up in the principal entrances, and set on fire in the hope that we should smoke the people out. The fire blazing in the trees all round grew hotter; the smoke was stifling, and there was no wind to drive it away; a drink of water would have been priceless; on every height near, the men were perched with their rifles ready. But all for nothing—no one bolted; and after we had tried to smoke them out for a couple of hours, word was brought that the robbers inside were talking to our own natives outside. It was true enough. We could hear their voices far down in the earth, quite comfortable, cool, and safe, telling us they would never come out, and that our fires did them no harm. There was no help for it: nature was against us, and we gave it up. The men were called off, and the robbers told they had better be out of the place by to-morrow or we would blow them up. Hardly had we turned our backs before half-a-dozen of the rascals were dancing in derision on the topmost stones of the hill. What could be done against such incorrigibles!

Next day the Engineers expended many pounds of dynamite trying to blow in the caves, but with little success. The boulders resisted any except the heaviest charges, and when they did move, only left a fresh hole elsewhere. However, the fellows cleared out, owing to the explosions, and we recaptured all the stolen property at our leisure.

Manyonyoba himself escaped to a cave near the head of the valley; and we followed him with the irregular cavalry, catching his people some way from their retreat, towards which they bolted like rabbits. There was a good deal of firing on both sides, but with little effect, Manyonyoba falling from a rock and hurting himself severely, escaping capture only from not being recognised.

On another occasion, the troops from Luneberg came out

and attacked a cave on their own account. The firing was very heavy, and before they had advanced a dozen yards, the sergeant-major and a corporal were shot dead. The natives remained masters of the position, and the soldiers marched home again with their dead comrades.

It was useless to attempt any active measures against such people; so the column sat down in their midst and waited to starve them out. This happened before very long: the chief, Manyon-yoba, with his principal wife and prime minister, gave themselves up, and were lodged in the *laager* at Luneberg; his people followed suit, and were allowed to remain in their caves, pending instructions about their removal.

Chapter Nineteen
Life in the Column

The trees about the mission-station were a pleasant lounge during the heat of the day, and were carefully protected from damage. The houses were in ruins; all had been stripped, the wood-work burnt, and the roofs smashed in. The fences had been broken down, and the whole enclosure given up to desolation. In the road lay the church bell, in little bits; and on the other side of what was once a hedge stood the kitchen-stove, battered and rusty,—too heavy to have been stolen. The fire, which had burnt the houses, had scorched many of the trees. Not a soul came near the place save ourselves; it was as much deserted as if in a desert. One day we needed a dissel-boom to replace a broken one; and a small tree, which showed signs of the fire, was selected, and cut down for that purpose. That afternoon, an undersized man, in a badly-fitting black coat, asked to see the colonel, and introducing himself as the owner of the station, presented a bill for £4,—the price of the tree which had been cut down, and of the stones from an old *cattle-kraal*, which we had taken to build round the graves by the river.

Luneberg, about four miles off, was another of those impositions which flourish in large letters as towns on maps of South Africa. It consists of five farms, within a circle of two miles, situated in, a grassy valley, embosomed in trees. Through the centre wanders a stream, and dotted about are *kraals* and "krantzes" of rocks, looking like more. Midway, where the soil is worn bare and dusty, stood two buildings,—the lower one the *laager*, surrounded by a high loop-holed wall; the other a fort, star-shaped, bristling with broken glass, and encircled by a tremendous ditch. In the former were collected the inhabitants of the district; they had taken the tilts off their waggons, and were comfortable enough, though somewhat crowded. Manyon-yoba had now joined the circle, and was doubtless more welcome there than when at large further off.

The farms are low, thatched buildings, substantially made of baked mud; each is shaded by a clump of blue-gums; a stream, with ducks and geese swimming about, is never far away. The front of the house is open to the road, without vestige of a fence, while behind will be a garden, the walks bordered with peach, fig, and mulberry trees,—these, in turn, often hung with granadillas. All except two of these farms were in ruins, and marked the limit of the Zulu raids.

While the column was in the valley of the Intombie, the rainy season set in, and for a week it poured day and night. That passed, and we had a succession of thunderstorms. First rolled up a bank of black vapour till the air is palpable and inky. Cloud follows cloud till night seems to have set in. A perfect stillness reigns. The horses foraging by the river collect in groups, with their heads from the coming storm. The swallows almost touch you as they skim along the ground. Tent-pegs are driven home, and tent-ropes loosened. Then, after some half-hour's suspense, comes a flash, rending the blackness, and from the rent issues a roll of thunder, which is taken up by the hills in dismal reverberations. A rush of wind follows, driving the dust in columns. The tents bulge and sway; some go down, everything movable rolls off before the gale. Then another flash, and a crash louder than the first. The wind redoubles its fury. A few spots of rain fall, and are followed by another flash, and a crash that deafens you. The air is filled with a roar, and with the hissing sound of rain. A grey wall advances down the valley. Hill-tops disappear behind it. The tall grass bends and springs up again, as if moved by electric shocks. Then the rain slashes down, and the earth flies up to meet it. Dry land becomes mud in a few minutes. Small torrents rush everywhere. The windows of heaven are opened, and it seems as if the land will disappear. Then a blinding flash, and the thunder echoes far into the mountains, rumbling and rolling till the next peal.

So the war of the elements goes on; fire, water, hurly-burly mingled, till the climax is reached, and the storm passes on to the next range. The valley it has travelled starts out green and refreshed, leaving grey wisps of vapour to hang about the gullies.

These storms are often circular, and are very puzzling to escape when met in the open.

In the spring, that is English autumn, they are generally the prelude of several days' rain. The earth is turned into a morass; lakes appear where yesterday the cattle were grazing; streams which ran over the sand-banks in the river's bed are torrents, hiding every trace of the bank you bathed from in the morning. Everything looks and feels wretched; for South Africa, where you live in the open air, requires fine weather to make it even bearable.

One of the most serious drawbacks to the colony is the absence of wood. Planks and beams have to be brought up from the coast at a great cost for conveyance. Poles, or dissel-booms, as they are called for waggons, which might be cut out of any ordinary tree, are worth a five-pound note in the Transvaal. A bamboo whip-handle fetches ten shillings. Firewood is equally scarce, so much so, that travellers camping out, miss that most welcome necessity in a camp, the camp fire.

About Luneberg, the mountains, and valleys between, were clothed with forests, a welcome sight after the treeless wastes of Zululand. Slangapies Berg, at the head of the valley where our camp lay, has wooded spurs running down to the Intombie, which in beautiful wildness are unequalled.

The flat-topped mountains divide the country into uplands, wide-spreading and grassy; and into valleys, cut up with *dongas*, stony and irregular. The uplands are glorious places, where the young grass is literally gemmed with flowers. Blue predominates, merging into purple. Great marigolds flaunt beside crimson zinnias; delicate harebells and lobelias lie hidden in the nooks. There are also semi-tropical flowers, quaintly shaped like brushes, or feathering plumes, gaudy in red and orange; tree-ferns live in the gorges where the streams are. You gaze for miles across a lawn, dipping to the rivulets, or rising to where piles of quartz-blocks lie jumbled together. These are called locally "*kopjies*," and are a sad impediment to travel. The view is magnificent, the lower country lying below like a map. From Slangapies Berg you look over Intabankulu and the Zlobane; further west Kambula; the mountains above Utrecht, and an endless series of "*kops*" and "*bergs*" stretch round towards the north. These ended, and the vast rolling plain of the Transvaal finishes the circle.

The one want is life. There are a few small birds and many hawks, but deer are wanting, and large game shy, and so manage to keep out of sight. Of men and women there is absolutely not a sign, and so stillness reigns unbroken.

No sooner do you leave the level ground to descend one of the spurs which lead below, than you come upon stones in countless numbers, scattered everywhere, hidden by the grass, but always so thick as to make riding difficult. Flat slabs, some yards across, pave the hillside; or else round boulders packed together leave unpleasant holes to slip into. What roads there are are cattle tracks, and wind about wonderfully; the oxen who made them just wandering on behind one another any "way they pleased, evidently with no eye for a straight line. Bogs are usual near the streams, and are nasty to cross, besides requiring experience to detect. Mealies have been grown on a patch of land scratched with a log of wood, and show that there are owners of the soil; but *kraals* are nowhere to be seen, the natives hereabout living in caves. After a long descent the stones increase, bushes grow up between the larger ones, the paving stones get flatter and more slippery, and make you think that it is time to dismount. All at once a gorge opens out on the right, the rocks which form its sides grey and precipitous, crumpled into a thousand fissures. Forest-trees hang down the face, tied together by "lianes" as thick as your leg; at the bottom are patches of level land of which the carpet is the greenest turf. Aloes and cacti, branching like candelabra, add a foreign element. Below all you hear the rush of water in the river. Many trees are of the order Poinsettia, their leaves bunches of scarlet, setting the foliage in a blaze of colour. Others are leafless, their branches clothed with scarlet flowers. Clumps of fresh spring green refresh the eye, and make the scene a little homelike. You lead your horse down a set of natural steps, and on reaching the bottom are aware that the inhabitants are not far off. Cocks are crowing, children laughing, and women mingle their shrill voices with the deeper tones of the men. A dog sends up a solitary bark, but as yet you see nothing but forest.

Exactly in front is a stream, its high banks clothed with fig-trees, the branches hanging over to the far side; and from these, as you ride up, drop a dozen little black urchins, and scamper away full speed. They run a couple of hundred yards and then dive suddenly into the thick underwood which grows at the base of a strangely isolated rock in the centre of the valley. As they approach this place the voices drop, dead silence ensues, and you feel that you are being looked at by a hundred invisible eyes. Then a chorus of dogs begins, and a flight of cocks and hens takes wildly to cover. A Kafir is seen stealing towards the same place, and is immediately cut off and brought to bay. He looks wild; half savage, half afraid, till we make friends by the present of a bit of tobacco, and the magic word "un-coco," fowls. He sets up a shout, and from the undergrowth startup the population, standing on the boulders or jumping on to others to obtain a better view. The boldest come out into the open, where they form line and watch us intently. Half-way up the rock, on a ledge almost hidden by brushwood, we can just distinguish their *kraals*. In front of them a wall breast-high has been built; the *kraals* themselves mark the entrances to caves, with which the hill is honeycombed. After more tobacco, we become friends and ride up to inspect. The urchins set up a shrill chorus and bolt under the rocks, but the men stand their ground. They are wild-looking people, most of them naked, some with a sheepskin thrown over their shoulders; all wear the "*moucha*." A little in rear are some females; the married women wearing a short petticoat of skin or sacking, black with age and dirt; the girls without exception stark naked, their ample proportions not even set off by a string of beads. Their faces were pretty; and their figures, innocent of stays, graceful and rounded. A Kafir belle moves with all the grace and elegance of her sex; infuses a spice of coquetry into her looks and actions;

and is all over the spoilt young lady, despite her nakedness, which is too absolute to be anything but innocent.

We give some more tobacco, and the boys start headlong after the fowls, who, wary by experience, run like race-horses, dodging under the rocks, or flying across the gully. But the boys are just as active, and jump about among the boulders most marvellously, till the unfortunates are pumped, and give themselves up with screams and cackling. The dogs join in the row, and are silenced by a volley of stones, aimed as only a Kafir knows how. The women advance and beg for tobacco; the men bring the captured fowls, holding out both palms for the money. We give some parting nods, and ride away down the valley, carrying tomorrow's dinner at our saddle-bows.

The presence of our column had its effect, and signs of peace became everywhere apparent.

Groups of natives were frequent, carrying bundles of sticks with which to rebuild their *kraals*; and some, bolder than the rest, ventured daily into camp with a few pots of dirty milk, or some skinny cocks and hens.

A young officer who had just come back from a patrol, was telling me of the success he had met with in dealing with the people, and said that he had purchased six fowls from one cave. "Of course," he added, "I paid for them, just to show that the business was genuine."

"How much did you give for them?" I asked.

"Oh, a shilling for the whole lot."

On the strength of his bargain he invited me to dine with him on one of the twopenny fowls. Now dinners in camp were only given when a special inducement could be held out. I have known one accepted on no better bait than a tin of lobster; but that was in Zululand before Ulundi. So great a dainty as a fowl, therefore, came like that well-advertised pen—"as a boon and a blessing to men,"—and was thankfully accepted. No time was wasted over formalities in these camp festivities; and the night of the dinner was the night of the day on which the invitation was issued. Punctual to time the guests arrived, and were met by the host with an apology that dinner would be half an hour late,—the wood was damp, and the fowl would not roast. So we sat on the boxes which were the seats, round the bigger one which was the table, and tried to be pleasant, notwithstanding the gnawing inside which the lateness of the dinner-hour brought about. Half an hour passed, then an hour, and the host waxed impatient. So the plates appeared. Ten minutes later we got a tin cup apiece, into which the soup was poured out of a saucepan, and dinner began. Coffee came next, — we were teetotallers in South Africa, and drank tea or coffee at every meal,—coffee with Swiss milk, and sugar black with dirt. Still, coffee in camp is warm and grateful, so each one mixed his and began to drink. We had no sooner tasted it than a general spluttering ensued; the host bolted outside, while we sat and tried to get rid of the taste with lumps of bread.

"What's the matter?" asked a sick boy in the corner, where he was lying up with fever.

"The matter is castor-oil, or something like it," we muttered.

"Oh," said the sick boy, "it's my servant, confound the fellow! Why, he's mixed the the coffee in the cup I've just taken the medicine in."

There was nothing left but to get on with the dinner, so the plates were swabbed and a tin of salmon produced; a dish of "trek-ox," curried, followed, which we partook of- sparingly, waiting for the fowl.

"Now, Barney, bring the fowl!" shouted the host.

"The fowl, sir?" said Barney in the doorway, evidently ready to bolt.

"Yes, stupid! the fowl that you've got for dinner."

"Oh, sir, the fowl's not cooked the night.'Twas a curry dinner you told me to do; and when it's a curry dinner, there's not enough pots to roast a fowl."

"No fowl!" gasped his master; "d'you mean to say there is nothing more to come?"

"Divil the ha'porth, your honour!" cried Barney, retreating just in time to miss his master's boot, and in the distance we heard his voice—

"Shure, sir, it's a misunderstanding between us; for the fowl's not aisy to cook, and you asking for a curry dinner."

After a time we calmed down, and made up for the fowl with a tin of raspberry-jam, washed down with "square-face," and then wished goodnight, and went off hungry to bed.

Chapter Twenty
Endings

The rolling plains of the Transvaal tempted us to ride across them. The road crosses the Intombie, and leads through a valley for the first ten miles, rising to the higher land by a series of well-marked terraces. Acres of fallen rock lay by the side of green turf; the cliffs were bright with foliage; streams cut through the soil; flowers were everywhere. In a dell, green and beautiful, we came upon a white man's skeleton: how it got there no one could tell. To the left was the farm of the "field-cornet" of the district, who was able to sell us a little butter and milk,—very delicious after months of abstinence. His daughter, a strapping girl of sixteen, was the first white woman we had seen. She had a strange way of coming straight up to you with her hand outstretched, looking you full in the face, without speaking, which was a little trying. Still she was a woman, though a Dutch one; so we took her hand, shaking it warmly, and watched her retire at once to the furthest corner of the room, where she lay in wait till the next arrival gave her the opportunity of commencing the operation over again.

The rounded hills, covered with grass, were dotted with the waggons of Boers, living in them and tending their herds of cattle or sheep. Their families were with them, — the women swathing their faces in napkins to preserve their complexions, and wearing sun-bonnets, just as our own girls do in haymaking-time. The men, when not surly, were familiar. I was sitting on the blankets in my tent one morning, putting on my clothes, when in stalked two hulking fellows in corduroys and slouch-hats. "Goot morning, captain!" they exclaimed, holding out their hands, which had to be duly shaken. After that they made themselves comfortable on the ground in front of me, filling their pipes and asking questions: "Where was Cetewayo? Was he still on his farm? Was he going to fight again, or not? Where did all the soldiers come from? We thought they were all killed at Isandlwana. Were any more coming up? Was the Transvaal to come back to the Dutch? We heard so. Dat is a fine gun; how much did it cost? I can shoot but with the rifle. I will show you; and I can hit anything."

On this the pair got up and began firing at an ant-hill, which they managed to miss as often as they let off. They evidently thought much of the title of captain, every question they asked finishing off with it. Then came more handshaking; and they went away.

The Transvaal soon becomes wearisome, there is so much sameness in its features: you live in the centre of a saucer of green turf,—everywhere is the rim above you, shutting out all beyond; there are no views,—to use the word landscape would be to misapply a well-known term: a bush, a shrub, or a rock would be pleasant variations. You do see a herd of "springbuck" about—and little piles of bones shine very white, and mark the place where hundreds of the same have been shot; but beyond this there is nothing but grass.

A return to camp was not without objections. Our cattle, always numerous, had a habit of falling sick and dying. The cause of this generally was lung-sickness, a complaint peculiar to South Africa. An ox attacked by it refuses, from sheer inability, to draw, and is left to die by the wayside. This does not mean, as in England, a corner under a hedge, in a lane where help can be given if needed. The way in South Africa is a track cut across a plain which extends for miles to the horizon; and the ox left to die by this wayside wanders hopelessly till he becomes a dot in the distance. If you are in camp thereabouts you will probably see the same dot in the same place for days. The grass is as good there as anywhere else, and the poor sick thing cannot eat it, bad or good, so it stands mournfully till it bethinks it of water. It essays to move, and as likely as not falls from sheer exhaustion and dies where it stood. If it has strength left, it paces off to the nearest stream and enters eagerly. The water is cool, the bank shelves easily, and it is soon breast-high; but in its sickness it has forgotten the mud at the bottom; its poor weak legs sink in, its back disappears, and it is lucky indeed if it can keep its nostrils sufficiently above for air. It must die at last, and poison the stream with its carcass. So our camps become surrounded by pestilential spots, drained by putrid water, and thoroughly unwholesome the longer we remained in one. Not a stream near that was not filthy with decaying bodies: the Pongola on its sand-banks had them by dozens, and the stench was fearful. Now and again would be brought in a few horses or mules recovered from the Zulus, all covered with mange and eaten up with sores; and it was a question how to get rid of them again. One redeeming point was the abundance of mushrooms which sprang up after the rains and made the land quite white in many places. They proved most excellent eating, and the soldiers stewed them with everything. Unluckily when we tried them ourselves, the solitary frying-pan in our canteens had got so thoroughly saturated with grease, from constant use, that the delicate flavour of the fungus was quite lost in the presence of stale fat.

We had been teetotallers for so long now that the wish for anything stronger than tea or coffee had gone, except in the evenings, when we sat on our beds and tried to talk. In Zululand the evenings had been too short and ourselves too tired for conviviality; lights had been put out punctually a little after eight, and we had to go to bed. Now the rule was relaxed and the evenings were very dull without books, chairs, and a glass of grog. Our only literature was an occasional local newspaper, and the contents of these, if not irritating, were commonplace. I remember reading a letter from a correspondent in the Transvaal belonging to a society called, so he said, "Ye Pretoria Twirlers" (a very appropriate title), complaining that the "Twirlers" were either living under a military despotism, or that a long Latin sentence, which he gave as a quotation, had been written with reference to the Governor, who had objected to the performance of certain personalities indulged in by the society. Had his Excellency been only gifted with the most ordinary common-sense he would have taken no notice. It appears that he did object to "an entertainment in which the Government was insulted or held up to ridicule," and, in consequence, had to learn that "if such proceedings had taken place under the sway of his Despotic and Autocratic Majesty the Emperor of all the Russias, one could have understood it; but that it should happen to subjects of the most free and liberally governed country on the globe is scarcely credible."

A Natal paper attending, through another correspondent, the weekly auction held in the Market Square, witnesses "a sight which causes us to reflect deeply upon the great mystery of death. There, on a stall, ranged, amid bottles of sweet nitre, Eno's fruit-salt, and kindred commodities, are the kits of men killed in the late war. What especially attracts our notice is a collection of the late Captain and gazing at the relics of this gallant officer, one is irresistibly reminded of how bravely he fell. He died a glorious death, and we feel grieved that his various household goods are lying in an open market. Here are his hunting top-boots, rather mouldy now, in which he has followed the hounds with all the ardour of youthful enthusiasm. There lie a pair of patent-leather shoes, in which he has danced, doubtless many a time, in the splendid mansions of the aristocracy; while round about are scattered neck-ties, white kid gloves, collars, uniforms, boot-trees, and other miscellaneous articles,—all of which speedily find purchasers amongst the crowd surrounding the auctioneer, who every few minutes impresses upon his audience the fact that these articles had really been the property of the gallant captain."

With such reading as our only resource, eked out with stringy beef and cold tea, it was no wonder that we heard with pleasure the column was to be broken up. Baker Russell was at Utrecht doing all he knew to enlist fresh drivers for a contemplated advance against Sekukuni in the far north, the old lot utterly refusing to go another step.

"You engaged us," they said, "to drive your waggons for a month, and when we had done that, you told us we must go on driving your waggons for another month; we did that too, and you would not let us go—and that is six months past; and you gave us no pay, and tell us that we can't go home, but must drive your waggons to that bad man Sekukuni. We are not like you; we can't write our words on paper: and so our wives, not seeing us come back, will think that we are dead, and will marry again; so that when you let us go, and we return to our homes, we shall find other men living in our *kraals*."

The Dragoons went off into the Transvaal to look after the Boers, who had talked themselves troublesome. Harness's battery, which had been present at Isandlwana, and had been with us ever since, left for the same place; while Darcy, with the Frontier Light Horse and the rest of the Irregulars, made for Utrecht to be disbanded. It was somewhat sad to part—for we had been together so long, and a campaign is the best of all schools for teaching men each other's worth. There is so much real work, and so many times when your own courage is animated by seeing that of the man next to you, that you are apt to feel for one another a deeper friendship than usual. Every one has the same aim,—the wish to beat the enemy; the hope that no one that he knows may be killed. In the Zulu war the disappointments had been very great, and they had been shared alike by every one in the field.

We had left England in a hurry; our property had been sold for a mere song; our relatives had barely time to say good-bye. On the passage our one topic was the time which would elapse between our landing and our first brush with the Zulus. We calculated that it would take us ten days to reach the Tugela, and that fighting would commence at once; a month from then would settle the whole business; and we knew that the transports which had brought us out had been engaged for three months to take us home again.

It was a bright prospect to be so sadly dimmed; and had any one ventured to hint that it would be two months after landing before we put our foot into Zululand, and three before we got a fight out of its people, he would have been laughed at. Yet that came to be the truth, —and more than that, no sooner had we got through our decisive fight at Ulundi, than we were told that the campaign would only then commence in earnest.

But after such disappointments, it speaks highly for the

training which a campaign gives to men, that when we separated it was with feelings of genuine regret, and with the plesantest memories of all those we had met in South Africa.

ALSO FROM LEONAUR
AVAILABLE IN SOFT OR HARD COVER WITH DUST JACKET

EW15 EYEWITNESS TO WAR SERIES
THE COMPLEAT RIFLEMAN HARRIS
by Benjamin Harris

The Adventures of a Soldier of the 95th (Rifles) During the Peninsular Campaign of the Napoleonic Wars.

SOFTCOVER : **ISBN 1-84677-047-5**
HARDCOVER : **ISBN 1-84677-053-X**

EW14 EYEWITNESS TO WAR SERIES
ZULU 1879
Selected by D.C.F Moodic & the Leonaur Editors.

The Anglo-Zulu War of 1879 from Contemporary Sources; First Hand Accounts, Interviews, Dispatches, Official Documents & Newspaper Reports.

SOFTCOVER : **ISBN 1-84677-044-0**
HARDCOVER : **ISBN 1-84677-051-3**

RC1 REGIMENTS & CAMPAIGNS SERIES
THE EAST AFRICAN MOUNTED RIFLES
by C.J.Wilson

Experiences of the Campaign in the East African Bush During the First World War (Illustrated).

SOFTCOVER : **ISBN 1-84677-042-4**
HARDCOVER : **ISBN 1-84677-059-9**

EW12 EYEWITNESS TO WAR SERIES
THE ADVENTURES OF A LIGHT DRAGOON IN THE NAPOLEONIC WARS
by George Farmer & G.R. Gleig

A Cavalryman During the Peninsular & Waterloo Campaigns, in Captivity & at the Siege of Bhurtpore, India.

SOFTCOVER : **ISBN 1-84677-040-8**
HARDCOVER : **ISBN 1-84677-056-4**

LEONAUR

ALSO FROM LEONAUR
AVAILABLE IN SOFT OR HARD COVER WITH DUST JACKET

EW13 EYEWITNESS TO WAR SERIES
THE RED DRAGOON
by W. J. Adams

With the 7th Dragoon Guards in the Cape of Good Hope Against the Boers & the Kaffir Tribes During the 'War of the Axe' 1843-48.

SOFTCOVER   : **ISBN 1-84677-043-2**
HARDCOVER   : **ISBN 1-84677-057-2**

MC2 THE MILITARY COMMANDERS SERIES
THE RECOLLECTIONS OF SKINNER OF SKINNER'S HORSE
by James Skinner

James Skinner & his 'Yellow Boys' Irregular Cavalry in the Wars of India Between the British, Mahratta, Rajput, Mogul, Sikh & Pindarree Forces.

SOFTCOVER   : **ISBN 1-84677-061-0**
HARDCOVER   : **ISBN 1-84677-071-8**

RC1 REGIMENTS & CAMPAIGNS SERIES
THE EAST AFRICAN MOUNTED RIFLES
by C. J. Wilson

Experiences of the Campaign in the East African Bush During the First World War (Illustrated).

SOFTCOVER   : **ISBN 1-84677-042-4**
HARDCOVER   : **ISBN 1-84677-059-9**

EW6 EYEWITNESS TO WAR SERIES
BUGLER & OFFICER OF THE RIFLES
by William Green & Harry Smith

With the 95th (Rifles) During the Peninsular & Waterloo Campaigns of the Napoleonic Wars.

SOFT COVER   : **ISBN 1-84677-020-3**
HARD COVER   : **ISBN 1-84677-032-7**

AVAILABLE ONLINE AT
www.leonaur.com
AND OTHER GOOD BOOK STORES

Printed in the United Kingdom
by Lightning Source UK Ltd.
113805UKS00002B/15